Ceramic Fish, Mermaids &

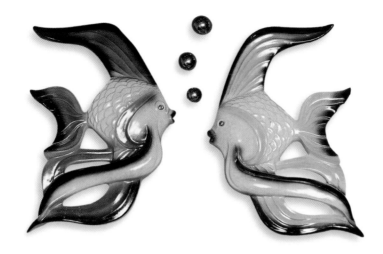

Bathroom Decorations of the 1940s & 1950s

Schiffer Publishing Ltd

Arleen Smith

4880 Lower Valley Road, Atglen, PA 19310 USA

Credits

Photography by Stephen Browning, Stephen's House of Photography, Turlock, CA

Pricing

The prices in this book should be used only as a guide. As with most collectibles, prices vary in different areas

Designed by Bonnie M. Hensley
Cover design by Bruce M. Waters
Type set in Zurich Blk BT/ZapfHumnst BT

ISBN: 0-7643-1337-1
Printed in China
1 2 3 4

Published by Schiffer Publishing Ltd.
4880 Lower Valley Road
Atglen, PA 19310
Phone: (610) 593-1777; Fax: (610) 593-2002
E-mail: Schifferbk@aol.com
Please visit our web site catalog at **www.schifferbooks.com**
We are always looking for people to write books on new and related subjects. If you have an idea for a book please contact us at the above address.

This book may be purchased from the publisher.
Include $3.95 for shipping.
Please try your bookstore first.
You may write for a free catalog.

In Europe, Schiffer books are distributed by
Bushwood Books
6 Marksbury Ave.
Kew Gardens
Surrey TW9 4JF England
Phone: 44 (0) 20 8392-8585; Fax: 44 (0) 20 8392-9876
E-mail: Bushwd@aol.com
Free postage in the U.K., Europe; air mail at cost.

Dedication

This book is dedicated to my wonderful husband, Art, who encouraged me in this endeavor and did the many hours of word processing work necessary to pull this collector's book together. What a sweetheart!

Acknowledgments

I am deeply grateful to the following people for their friendship, their encouragement and their support of my "gone fishing" project:

My son, Steve, who has become quite a "fisherman" for me in antique stores and swap meets in southern California. My son, Shad, who does his "fishing" the easy way, in *my* collection, to decorate his home in northern California. My daughter, Sheri, and our four Grandkids, Shanna, Stacia, Matthew, and Sarah, for guiding me on many of my "fishing" trips in Colorado. And, my parents, Wayland and Thelma Morrison for helping me find a few of the best "fishing spots," in the Pacific Northwest.

I also want to thank: Rosemarie & John LaBelle, Old Hotel Antiques, Sutter Creek, California; Delores & Dan Dean, Manhattan Trading Post, Sherwood, Oregon; Shirley Konze, The Blue Lupine Antiques, Sutter Creek, California; Dottie and Linzy Cotham, Back in Time, Roseville, California; Nancy and Tully Bryant, B's Balderdash, Pine Grove, California; Lyndy and Tim Pickens, Vallejo, California; Marty Frasinetti, Sacramento, California; and our photographer, Stephen Browning, Turlock, California.

And lastly, my No.1 supporter, my husband, Art. He has gone "fishing" with me countless times and has developed a keen eye for ceramic sea creatures. But the most memorable was when, on his own, he spent the entire day "fishin'" for me. He "caught" one fish. In the back of the book you'll see the "treasure" he found. This has to be the most pathetic-looking little yellow fish in the entire fish world. It should have gotten away and it doesn't look like much, but it is now among my most valued treasures.

Special Acknowledgment

Thanks must go to our many early California potters whose artistic works were created all along the coast of southern California. I was fortunate to grow up among these artisans. And we must not forget the talented and creative artisans in Japan, who were major contributors to these wonderful collectibles.

Contents

Introduction

California Pottery and Made in Japan

There are few collectibles that so vividly mark a period in our American history as do the colorful ceramic fish, bubbles, mermaids and seahorses of the 1950s and 1960s. The popularity of these bathroom decorations literally swept the country and became a fad that would be remembered for years to come. They were the creation of gifted artists, ceramic designers and pottery makers, who made their home and established their business in California, and more specifically, southern California. Southern California's warm and temperate climate, its laid-back lifestyles, its sunny beach communities and the glamour and lure of Hollywood, attracted and won the hearts of the artisans, who chose to live and to work in such a desirable environment.

Many of the most famous and talented designers and manufacturers of what is now known as "California pottery" launched their careers in the small beach and inland communities of southern California. Such well-known designers and ceramic pottery makers as Kay Finch. Freeman-McFarlin, Hedi Shoop, Josef Originals, DeForest, and Ceramicraft were among the companies whose businesses flourished there. In addition, there were countless numbers of smaller producers, who started well-intentioned, but all too often short-lived, ceramics businesses as hobbies or avocations, in their homes or garages.

Another factor that contributed to the attraction and popularity of southern California for pottery makers was that the raw material needed for their craft could be easily and inexpensively obtained in the area and its vast desert region would contribute one of its treasures important to the industry: talc.

It was estimated that there were over 800 potteries in southern California during the height of the ceramic fish, bubbles, mermaids and seahorses fad of the 1950s. During this time, and for many years hence, these wonderful decorations were sold in pottery shops and yards, 5 and 10 cent stores, department stores, and gift shops, and could be found in home bathrooms not only in California but throughout the United States and Canada. Almost everyone during that era had a set of ceramic fish, or knew of someone, a mother, an aunt, or a grandmother, who had a set decorating their bathroom. Perhaps they still do. Without a doubt, they truly represent 1950s Americana.

The popularity and collectibility of California pottery continued to grow over the years as did the fame and recognition of the industry's most talented designers. Little did they know that their work would literally change the face of pottery and ceramic art and create a legacy of collectibles for generations to come.

Japanese pottery imports had a dramatic impact upon the United States in the years following the American occupation of Japan after World War II. The favorable yen-to-the-dollar exchange rate made manufacturing in Japan very desirable, compared to the much higher costs of U.S. manufacture. Thus, there were several companies in the U.S. that opted to import ceramic giftware from Japan. Companies such as Lefton, Napco, and Norcrest China Co., bear the "Made in Japan" markings. Josef Originals also succumbed to the need to lower manufacturing costs and moved their manufacturing and distribution to Japan.

Most of the pottery factories in Japan, as in California, were small, family-owned businesses. While the creative style of the pottery designers and artists in Japan differs from those in the U.S., and are easily recognizable, they are nonetheless equally popular and collectible. As the imports from Japan began to flood the U.S. market, only the strongest of the California potteries were able to compete and, to their credit, their product quality was never compromised. However, by the mid 1960s most of the smaller U.S. potteries were gone, unaware that their creative and artistic efforts would not be forgotten – that their brightly-colored fish and bubbles, and the beautiful mermaids, with their flowing-hair and the cute, frolicking seahorses, would live on through the ages and bring timeless enjoyment and rewards to collectors of all ages.

"Gone Fishing"

A Guide To A Wonderful And Fun Collectible

I am anxious to share with you the most enjoyable collection I have ever had! It is a collection of ceramic sea life, brilliant-colored and playful fish, adorable mermaids, and graceful seahorses, in a variety of wall hangings and decorative wall pockets.

When I say that it is the most enjoyable collection I have ever had, I say it, admittedly, as a confirmed, addicted, dedicated, card-carrying, collectible collector! I love collecting! I love prowling and searching through all manner of antique shops and malls, flea markets, street fairs, garage and estate sales, auctions, grungy surplus stores and dusty old thrift shops.

Like Pavlov's dog, I am almost to the point of salivating at the mere mention of an upcoming show or sale, or when I am driving through a new town that I haven't scouted thoroughly from one end to the other.

From the very beginning, this collection has been the source of hours upon hours of enjoyment, entertainment and smiles for my entire family. You might ask, "Did you say smiles?" That's right. Once you start your collection, I'm certain you will find it virtually impossible to look at them, see their variety of cute and animated expressions, and picture in your mind's-eye their antics without smiling. You'll catch yourself time-and-again, as they almost magically create a feeling of contentment, happiness, and well being.

As my collection was developing, my nightly greeting to my husband, home from his workday, would include, "Want to see my new fish?" I would then proudly show him my acquisitions and rearrangements "du-jour."

to by my family as a "clean freak," not to an extreme, but I do admit to wanting to keep our home neat and tidy. But, I'll also admit that there have been times, not too often, when my "tidying" resulted in things being inadvertently discarded, when they shouldn't have been. Today, I realize that too many things found their way into church thrift shops or into the trash can because they were thought to be no longer serviceable or usable. They were old and dusty and taking up valuable space. We replaced the old with new. And, gradually the old disappeared, in garage sales or given to the Salvation Army.

My penchant for "when in doubt, throw it out" is deep-seated, but let me tell you, when you have three children and a husband, and all of them possessing a strong propensity for saving everything, it explains an occasional nocturnal vision of living in a house piled high, from floor to ceiling, with antiques of all shapes and sizes. In my dream there was only a narrow path, body-width, that made a maze-like corridor to move from room to room. Thankfully, I would awaken to reality, but with a renewed conviction not to let that happen to my house!

My collection includes literally hundreds of fish, mermaids, and seahorses of various colors and sizes, along with assorted other sea creature things, like seashells that are salt & pepper shakers, star fish, and a "bajillion" bubbles.

Each of my fish, mermaids, and seahorses, unlike other collectibles I have happily acquired, have taken on individual personalities. Some of their expressions seem to tell a story (a "fish story" maybe?) with their different sizes, shapes, and colors, and the shiny-bright bubbles.

Other collectibles you may want to add to your collection of ceramic sea creatures, as I have, include a wide variety of ceramic salt and pepper shakers in the shapes of fish, mermaids, seashells, shells, starfish, crabs, lobsters, etc. They are made in many colors and sizes and make a beautiful addition to your collection and arrangements.

I do feel that I must warn you, right up front, collecting these ceramic sea-creatures can be incurably addictive, but I'm confident they will prove to be a wonderful investment of your time and treasure.

How On Earth Did All This Get Started?

Collecting for me started rather late in my life. I am truly one of those living, breathing, examples of the old adage, "too soon old, too late smart!" If the truth were known, I was always the antithesis of collecting. I was, from as far back as I can remember, a bonafide "thrower-outer!" When in doubt, throw-it-out! Sometimes to my family's dismay.

By way of explanation, I've sometimes been lovingly referred-

But, oh, how I wish that I had started collecting as a child or as a teenager, or that I had developed an early gift of foresight and had put away the toys and the baseball cards and the many, many mementos and keepsakes in a safe place, etc. So many of those things are today considered priceless treasures and highly-collectible, valued in the hundreds, if not thousands of dollars.

Thankfully, among the few things that survived my "throw-out-itis" was a prized bathroom decoration that consisted of a set of three ceramic fish, three wonderful ceramic mermaids, and three gold bubbles! One of the fish was a big wall pocket that went together with two cute little matching fishies. They had a special place in my heart, because I had purchased them for Art's and my first home. It wasn't any clairvoyance or feminine intuition some 40 plus years ago that made me carefully wrap and store them away. I didn't know what collecting and collectibles were at that time. I just liked them a lot and I wanted to save them.

With my ceramic fish and mermaids safely stored and out of sight, I hadn't thought about them for years and I might not have thought about them for years to come, if it hadn't been for an antique dealer friend, whose name is Laura. I had stopped by her home with a few pieces of depression glass that I found for her. As we chatted, she mentioned that she would also like for me to be on the lookout for ceramic fish and mermaids. I thought at the time, "ceramic fish and mermaids? I used to have some cute fish and mermaids on my bathroom wall!" Laura took me into her bathroom to show me what she was looking for and all of a sudden, as I looked at her wall filled with little fish and mermaids, my mind went instantly back to the ones I had saved and put away so many years ago, but I had no idea where they were.

That evening, I couldn't think of anything else. Where were those fish? I remembered that I had seen them about 15 years earlier when our family was packing to move up to the beautiful foothills of Northern California. I couldn't wait to get home to begin my "treasure hunt!"

For the next few days I thought of little else. When I found them, it was like finding a long-lost friend or opening that very special gift on Christmas morning. I was overjoyed!

My first thought was, "I can't give these up, they have special meaning to Art and to me." I showed them to Art and we talked about the wonderful memories of the early 50s, and thoughts about how I, as a young bride, had bought the fish and mermaids to decorate our first new home. I just couldn't give them up. However, I did start to look for other fish and mermaids for Laura.

At first, I would find three or four of the ceramic sea creatures for Laura and I would keep one for myself. Before long, I was keeping four or five for me and taking only one to Laura. I found that in my sea creature "fishing," it wasn't the fish that "got hooked." It was me!

Things To Watch For

As your collection grows, you'll see that the majority of the highest quality fish and other sea creatures are made by ceramic manufacturing facilities located in southern California. Other high quality pieces are made by companies in Japan.

As a word of caution, it is well to avoid pieces that are made by amateur moldmakers and amateurs in ceramics. You will find that for the most part they are quite easy to spot. They are usually heavier and more often than not, poorly painted. The pieces made by the pros are lighter in weight, have more detail in both the mold and in the painting and their colors are far more vibrant. If you do end up with one that is of lesser quality, don't fret. Just put it in your next garage sale.

Identifying Markings

Most of the sea creatures you will find have manufacturer's markings on the back that identifies their origin. These markings will often include their company name, product-identifying numbers and in some cases, the country in which they were made. The methods of marking their products include:

Paper labels, attractive, but not permanent.
Rubber or ink stamps, applied before the last firing.
Silk screen imprints, a very clean and neat mark with an embossed look.
Carved or stamped mold markings, achieved by carving directly into the mold.
Transfer, applied before firing. After the firing, this method would leave a clean, permanent mark.

Many of the products have no identifying marks. Quite possibly these were originally marked with paper labels which are not as permanent as those markings that are carved or stamped into the molds. Products that are ink stamped, or those imprinted by a silk screen method and then oven-glazed, retain their identity marks while many of the paper labels were washed away, pealed off, or, over the years, lost their sticking ability and fell off. Still others could only be identified by the markings on their original shipping or packing boxes.

Manufacturers/Distributors

Of Ceramic Fish, Mermaids & Seahorses

A Partial Listing:

Bradley Exclusive, Japan
Ceramicraft, San Clemente, California
CNC, Los Angeles & Japan
Deforest of California, Duarte, California
Duran's Royal, California
Enesco, Japan, Elk Grove Village, Illinois
Erickson's, California
Freeman-McFarlin Originals, El Monte, California
Gayrt
Gilner, Culver City, California
Grayson Arts, California
Hedi Schoop, North Hollywood, California
Irene Smith, California
Japan Design Center, Japan
Josef Originals, Monrovia, California/Japan
Joty, USA (believed to be California)
Kay Finch, Corona Del Mar, California
Kelvin, Exclusives Japan
Lefton's Exclusives, Japan
Marroco-Decor, Japan
Nameth Entp., Made in California - Distributor
Napco Ceramic, Japan
Norcrest China Company, Portland, Oregon,
Pandora Potteries, Santa Monica, California
PY, Japan
Semco, Japan
S.L. Cluter
Tropic Treasures by Ceramicraft, San Clemente, California
UCAGCO/United China and Glass Co. Inc., Japan

I'm sure more manufacturers and distributors of ceramic fish and other sea creatures will be discovered after the publishing of this first book. I would be grateful for any input and will be happy to include them in future printings.

CERAMICRAFT and TROPIC TREASURES BY CERAMICRAFT

Located in San Clemente, California, Ceramicraft was among the largest producers of ceramic sea creatures in the U.S. There is little information currently available about this company or affiliated companies, and their talented artists. Their adorable little sea creatures are recognizable with their brilliant colors and Disney-like expressions. I make this comparison because it seems that every time I look at the expressions on many of the old Disney cartoon animals, or at the Ceramicraft & Tropic Treasures sea creatures, I get similar, happy feelings.

Ceramicraft manufactured and distributed literally hundreds of fish in a variety of sizes, colors, wall pockets, and wall hangings. Some were singles, but most were in groups. I have also found a variety of other ceramics made by this company. It appears that their most prolific production years were in the 1950s and probably ended in the early 1960s

The majority of Ceramicraft's products are identified by an ink stamp; however, the design of the stamp was changed several times. I was surprised to find that a few of their gift-boxed products had no identifying mark, other than the box. (See photo in Section One) For a short period of time a paper label was used and then replaced by a series of ink stamps.

If any of my readers has any additional information about this company I would appreciate hearing from you.

Note: Ink marks done before final firing.

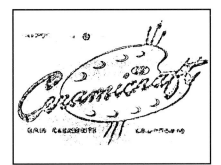

FREEMAN-McFARLIN

This company was started in El Monte, California, in 1927 by owner, Gerald McFarlin. It was known as McFarlin Potteries. In 1951, Maynard A. Freeman joined the company as a partner and its Chief Designer. Freeman's design of a new line of slip-cast earthenware sculpture propelled the company to new success. Ceramic fish and mermaids, birds, and many wild and domestic animals were produced by the company, along with a variety of other items.

In 1963 Freeman-McFarlin purchased all of Kay Finch's molds after she closed her company. Kay Finch was later commissioned by the company to design a few new animals, mostly dogs, that would be added to their lines.

McFarlin sold his interest in the late 1960s and Freeman sold out in 1972. The El Monte factory was closed in 1975.

ENESCO CORPORATION

Founded in 1959, by the N. Shure Company, a wholesale catalog merchandising company, to market giftware from the Orient, Enesco is today a major importer/distributor of giftware worldwide. Originally located in Chicago, on Lake Shore Drive, the company has enjoyed phenomenal growth under the leadership of CEO Eugene Freedman, and in the mid-1970s they moved to Elk Grove Village, just South of Chicago, near the O'Hare International Airport. Their catalogs, over the past years, include highly collectible giftware items such as glazed ceramic and semi-porcelain head vase planters, "Precious Moments" figurines, religious ware, and, most importantly for this publication, colorful sea creatures.

HEDI SCHOOP

Born in Germany, Hedi Schoop immigrated to the United States in 1933. She settled in North Hollywood, California, on Burbank Blvd. In 1940, with the financial assistance of her mother, she began what was to become one of the most successful "California pottery" careers of the 1940s and 1950s.

Hedi Schoop designed and molded most of the figurines that were produced by her company. In 1942 the company became known as Hedi Schoop Art Creations, which produced over 30,000 items annually. Her factory was destroyed by fire in 1958. Hedi decided not to rebuild and opted to do freelance work until she retired in the early 1960s. Most of her identifying marks were stamped.

Hedi Schoop
HOLLYWOOD CAL.

Hedi
Schoop

HEDI SCHOOP
CALIFORNIA

JOSEF ORIGINALS

This Arcadia, California-based company is known for their charming figurines of young girls and animals. The company was formed in 1946 by Muriel Joseph George. She was the chief designer until she retired in 1982. In the early 1960s, George Good became her partner and he persuaded her to produce figurines in Japan. Up until that time all of her work was produced in California. The product quality remained high. Josef Originals are marked with an oval sticker and indicate manufacture in either California or Japan. Those from Japan will be ink stamped Japan on the back and a small oval black & gold Japan sticker on the front. The spelling of "Josef" was actually a spelling error in the printing of the first labels and it stuck!

KAY FINCH

Kay Finch received her art training at Scripps College, in Claremont, California. It was during her studies with William Manker that he encouraged her to pursue pottery commercially. She located her studio in 1939 in Corona Del Mar, on the Pacific Coast Highway, along with her husband, who took care of the administrative business.

In 1940, Kay Finch pottery designs came into prominence with a highly successful series of cute little pigs. The popularity of her designs prompted the opening of a retail showroom in 1941.

Kay also had an intense interest in championship dog breeding, which had an obvious influence in her pottery work. Her successful pottery business came to an end in 1963, with the death of her husband; however, she continued to do some design work with the Freeman-McFarlin company.

KAY FINCH
CALIFORNIA

Kay Finch
Calif

LEFTON

George Zolton Lefton, was born in Hungary. He came to the United States and settled in Chicago, Illinois, in 1939. In 1941 he established his importing company, with the majority of his items coming from Japan. At the end of World War II Lefton was known, unofficially, as "The China King." Today, the Lefton's Exclusive Japan logo is well-known and respected by collectors and the company has become the leading distributor of ceramic giftware throughout the world.

UCAGCO/UNITED CHINA & GLASS CO., INC.

This importing company, under the name of Abe Mayer & Co., dates back to the mid 1800s, making it one of the oldest of the importing companies in the United States. The original company was reorganized in 1908 as the United China and Glass Co. Inc. It wasn't until 1935 that UCAGCO appeared as their trademark. After World War II, UCAGCO, with Mr. S.A. Stolaroff as their agent/designer, was the first U.S. company to import products from Japan. Stolaroff worked closely with the Japanese potters and was honored by the Japanese government, naming him one of the world's finest ceramic designers. Stolaroff retired in 1962.

NAPCO (NATIONAL POTTERIES CORPORATION)

Located in Bedford, Ohio, the importing company, NAPCO, was founded in 1938. Owned and operated by a Midwestern family, they import a variety of collectible ceramics along with other giftware.

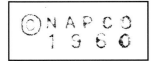

Other Companies and

Their Identifying Marks

BRADLEY EXCLUSIVE, Japan

Red foil label, gold lettering

NORCREST CHINA COMPANY

Originally founded in 1924, under the name Northwest Trading Company, by Hide Naito, this Oregon company imported low-priced ceramic giftware from Japan along with bone china from England. The company has relocated many times and each time to larger facilities. Their name was changed to the Norcrest China Company in 1955. Their identifying marks are primarily paper labels, however, the company was known to use a variety of marks.

CNC, Los Angeles & Japan

Gold foil, black background

DEFOREST OF CALIFORNIA, Duarte, California

Mold impression mark

Brown ink stamp

Black ink

DURAN'S ROYAL, California

Mold impression mark

ERICKSON'S, California

Gold foil, black in

GILNER, Culver City, California

Mold impression mark

GRAYSON ARTS, California

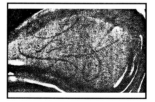

Gold foil, black ink

IRENE SMITH, California

Very light mold impression mark would not copy

JAPAN DESIGN CENTER, Japan

  Black ink stamp

JOTY, USA

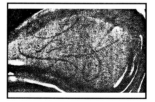

Script impression in mold

KELVIN EXCLUSIVES, Japan

Silver foil, black ink   Black ink stamp

MARROCO, Decor. Made in Japan

Silver foil with red lettering

NAMETH ENTERPRISES, Made in California

Gold foil, black lettering

S. L. CLUTER

Mold impression mark

PANDORA POTTERIES, Santa Monica, California

Light mustard yellow label, brown lettering

TROPIC TREASURES BY CERAMICRAFT

Silver foil label, black ink. Believed to be first mark of the company

PY JAPAN

Ink stamp, black or brown

SEMCO, Japan

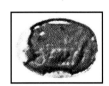 

Pressure stamped gold foil label

Section One

Ceramic Fish,
Mermaids & Seahorses

O.K., it's photo time.
Grab your fishing pole
and let's you and I go fishing!!

Kay Finch, California
Seahorses & Coral Fern, warm brown & gold. Large Seahorse 16-1/
2" tall; small Seahorses, 6" tall; Coral Fern 9" high. (Rare) Very fine
quality. $500-550 set.

Lefton's Exclusive, Japan
Mermaids (pair) sitting on seahorses. Pink/blue & pearl, jewel eyes in seahorses, 6-3/4" high. With bubbles. $180-190 pair

Opposite page
Top: **Stamped Japan**
Mermaids (doll-like) holding gold starfish, green tails. 6-1/2" tall, 4-1/2" long. $175-190 pair

Bottom: **Freeman-McFarlin**
Fish (pair). Yellow & pearl, 8" long, 7-1/2" high. With heart bubbles. $110-125 pair

Norcrest (P659), Japan
Mermaids holding fish (set of 3). 5-3/4" and 5" tall. Nice detail. With bubbles. $225-235 set

Py, Japan Center
Fish (pair). Cerise & green, jewel eye, 6-1/2" tall; blue & cerise, jewel eye, 7" tall. With heart bubbles. $95-100 pair

United China & Glass Co., Inc. (UCAGCO), Japan
Fish, large. Yellow & black, 10" long, 9-3/4" high. With bubbles. $75-80

Lefton Exclusive (3158), Japan
Mermaids (pair) on seahorses with original hanging tags marked "Designed by Marika." Red hair, green tail, 7-1/4" tall. With bubbles. $180-190 pair

Freeman-McFarlin Originals, El Monte, California
Fish (pair). Green/yellow/purple, iridescent pearlized colors (rare). 11-3/4" tall. With bubbles. $140-150 pair

Freeman-McFarlin Originals, El Monte, California
Fish. Aqua, 12-1/2" tall, 8" long (rare).
With bubbles. $70-75

United China & Glass Co., Inc. (UCAGCO), Japan
Fish. Blue, some Pink, with Black & Yellow stripe. Large, 9" tall. Unusually fine quality. $70-75

Norcrest (P-300), Japan
Mermaids (4). Green glitter tails, richly decorated with seashells, pearls, jewels, and more. 5-1/4" to 5-1/2" tall. $70-75 each

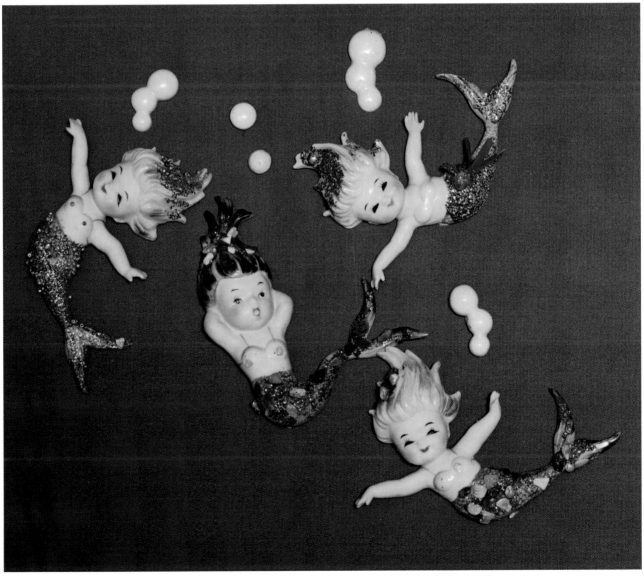

Lefton's Exclusive, Japan
Mermaids (pair). Green tail,
7-1/4" tall. With bubbles.
$180-190 pair

**Tropic Treasures by Ceramicraft,
California**
Pufferfish (rare). Pink & black, 7"
long. $70-75

Ceramicraft, San Clemente, California
Fish (set of 4). Yellow and black. Large wall pocket, 10-1/2"; medium, 6"; small, 5-1/2"; extra-small, 4". With gold bubbles. $110-125 set

There are times when I look at my fish, the little ones, the babies, along with the big ones, possibly the mommies, and I begin humming an old song that begins with the words, "Downin the meadow in the itty-bitty poo, swam three little fishies and the momma fishie too..."

Tropic Treasures by Ceramicraft, California
Fish (set of 4). Green & black. Large, 7-1/2" long; small, 4-1/2" long. With bubbles. $85-90 set

Hedi Schoop, Corona Del Mar, California
Fish (Rare). Light blue/black/silver, 8-1/2" long. "Hedi Schoop Calif. 472." Perfect condition. $100-125

Lefton, Japan
Mermaids (set of 3). Bisque with jewels, long red hair, and green tails.
Large, 8" tall; with bubble, 5" tall; with mirror, 5" long. With bubbles. $165-175 set

Kay Finch, California
Seahorse (rare). Aqua and gold,
16-1/2" tall. Very fine quality.
$250-275

Lefton, Japan
Mermaids (pair). Bisque, light green with
yellow tails. 8" tall. $180-190 pair

Tropic Treasures by Ceramicraft
Fish (set of 5). Yellow & black, Large, 11-1/2" long; small, 3-3/4" long; extra-small, 2" long. With gold bubbles. $125-135 set

Lefton's Exclusive, Japan (Small label)
Mermaid seated, with starfish. Pastel pink/yellow/blue & pearl. 7-1/2" tall. $85-90

Ceramicraft, San Clemente, California
Fish (group of 6). Pink & black, Large, 7.25″ long; small, 3-3/4″ long. With gold bubbles. $110-125 group

Japan
Fish (pair). Green & blue, 6-1/2″ tall, and pink & white, 6-1/4″ tall. With heart bubbles. $80-85 pair

Ceramicraft, San Clemente, California
Angelfish (set of 5). Blue & black. Large, 12-1/2" tall, 10-1/2" long; small, 7-1/4" tall, 6-1/2" long. With gold bubbles. $125-135 set

Japan
Mermaid with fish. Green tail, 4-3/4" tall. $65-70

No mark, Japan
Fish. Pink/yellow, 2-1/2" long. $10-12. Starfish/seashell salt & pepper, $15-18 pair

Freeman-McFarlin
Mermaids (set of 4), rare. Large, 8-1/2" tall; sitting on bubble, 6-1/2" tall; blowing bubble, 5" tall; holding bubble, 5-1/4" tall. With bubbles. $195-210 set

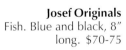

Josef Originals
Fish. Blue and black, 8" long. $70-75

Freeman-McFarlin
Fish. Brown & pearl, 7-1/2" long, 8-1/2" high. With bubbles $50-55.
Starfish and seashell salt & pepper shakers, $15-18 set

Top right: **Lefton Exclusive, Japan**
Mermaids sitting in seashells (pair). Green tails, 7" tall. $180-195 pair

Freeman-McFarlin
Fish (set of 4). Pink/green/purple. Large wall pocket, 8" tall; small, 2-1/2" long. With bubbles. $90-95 set

Lefton's Exclusive, Japan
Mermaid with seahorses (rare). Purple tail, seahorses blue/white & purple/white. Lefton's 2223. $110-125

Norcrest (P659), Japan
Mermaids holding fish (pair). Blue tails with glitter, blond & red hair. $150-160 pair

Lefton's Exclusive, Japan
Fish (pair). Blue & pearl, pink & pearl, 6" tall. $110-125 pair

Royal Bayreuth
Spiky shell salt & pepper shakers. Blue & white satin pearl finish. $140-160 pair

DeForest of California, Duarte, California
Mermaids. Warm brown & gold tails. Large, 6" long; small, 3" long.
With bubbles. $115-125 set

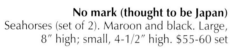

No mark (thought to be Japan)
Seahorses (set of 2). Maroon and black. Large,
8" high; small, 4-1/2" high. $55-60 set

Japan
Fish (2 sets). Pink/yellow. Large, 6-1/4" long; small, 3-1/4" long. One
large & 2 small per set. $55-60 set of 3

No mark
Frogs on lily pads, wall plaques. Green & white. $10-15 each

Joty
Mermaids (set of 4). Black tails, decorated with shells, jewels, and starfish, Large, 9" tall; mermaid with mirror and with harp, 5-1/2"; with arrow, 5-1/4". With bubbles. $175-185 set

Ceramicraft, San Clemente, California
Fish. Yellow and black. 8-1/2" long. With gold bubbles. $32-36

Lefton's Exclusive (#528), Japan
Mermaid on seahorse. Red tail, blond hair on black/gold seahorse, 7" long, with fish, blue/white, 1" long. $95-110 set

Japan (KWS 0153)
Mermaids diving (set of 3). Green tails. Large, red hair, 4-1/2" high; small, light brown hair, 3-3/4" high. With bubbles. $120-130 set

No mark
Fish (set of 4). Pink & black. Large, 4-3/4"; small, 3-1/2". With gold bubbles. $65-70 set

Ceramicraft, San Clemente, California
Fish (set of 5). Pink & black. Large wall pocket, 8-1/2" long; medium, 6-1/2"; medium-small, 5-3/4"; small, 4-1/2"; extra-small, 3" long. With bubbles. $125-135 set

Lefton Exclusive, Japan
Mermaids (set of 3). Large mermaid with blond hair & green tail, 9" tall; small mermaid, blond hair, 4-1/4" tall. With bubbles. $155-165 set. Mermaid with two seahorses, 4-1/4" tall. $100-110

Japan
Mermaids with parasols. Yellow, green, and pink. 5-1/2" tall. Parasols are 3" x 6". $85-95 each

43

Ink-stamped Japan
Fish (set of 3). Pink, green, yellow, black.
Large, 6" long, 7-1/2" high; small, 3" long,
3-1/2" high. With bubbles. $65-70 set

Ceramicraft, San Clemente, California
Fish (set of 5). Brown & pearl, jewel eyes. Large, 8-
1/2" long, small, 5-1/4" long. With white/gold
bubbles. $135-145 set

Norcrest (P52), Japan
Mermaid soapdish. Pink/gold tail, pearl soapdish.
9" tall. $95-110

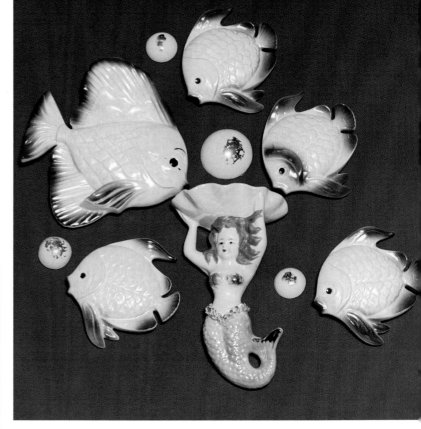

DeForest of California, Duarte, California
Flyingfish (rare). Pink & gold, jewel eyes. Large,
10-1/4" long; small, 4-1/4" long. With bubbles.
$75-85 pair

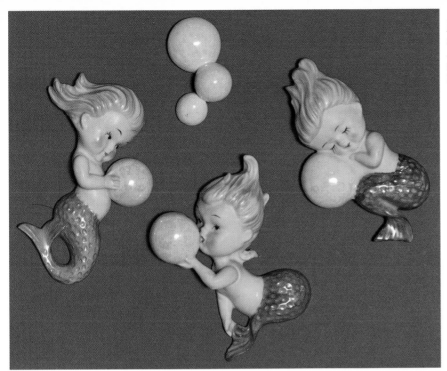

Japan
Mermaids. Purple tail, 4-1/4" tall; magenta, 5" tall; green, 5-1/4" long. Small red & gold sticker, "Made in Japan 2208 P-318." With bubbles. $195-205 set

Japan (#4489)
Mermaids sitting in shell (pair). Green tail, 7-1/4" tall. Small blue sticker, "Made in Japan." $165-175 pair

Norcrest (P300), Japan (Was also made in P360)
Mermaids (set of 3). Green sparkling tails, red, light brown & blond hair. With bubbles. $180-190 set

Bradley Exclusive, Japan
Mermaids (pair). Pink tail, blue tail, 6-1/2" tall. Tails have sand-like glass sprinkles. $140-150 pair

Py, Japan
Fish (rare). Light brown/gray & light blue, with black stripes. 7" long, 7-3/4" high. $70-75

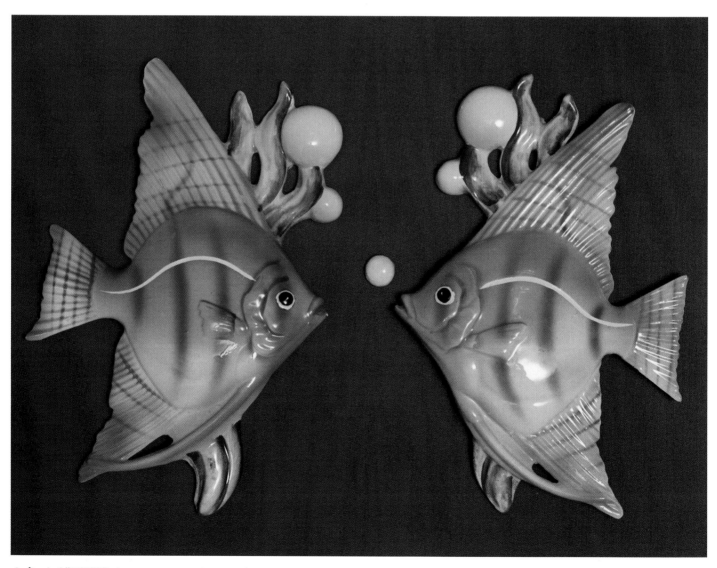

Lefton's (#2629N), Japan
Fish (pair). Pink and yellow, 8" high, 5-1/2" long. $100-110 pair

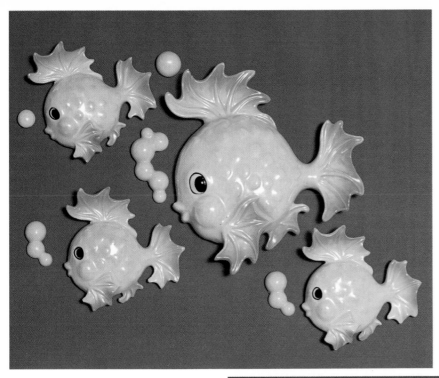

Ink-stamped Japan
Fish (set of 4). Pearl & apricot. Large, 6-1/2" long; small, 4" long. With bubbles. $110-125 set

Tropic Treasures by Ceramicraft, California
Fish (set of 4). Green & black. Large wall pocket, 9-1/2" long; medium, 5-3/4" long; small 3-1/4" long. With bubbles. $120-135 set

UCAGCO Py, Japan
Fish (pair), unusual and well made. Yellow & black. 7" long, 8-1/2" high. With bubbles. $100-115 pair

No mark
Seahorses (set of 3). Blue, decorated with jewels and glitter. Large 10-1/2" tall; medium, 6-3/4"; small, 3-1/4". With bubbles. $60-65. Starfish, $5-6 each.

No mark (has the look of DeForest)
Mermaid. Pink and gold tail, brown hair. 8-3/4" tall. $95-100

No mark (thought to be Joty)
Mermaids (set of 4). Light green & gold tail, artistically decorated with sea shells and jewels. Large, 9" tall; with mirror, 5-1/2"; with harp, 5-1/2"; with arrow, 5-1/4". With bubbles. $180-190 set

Japan
Fish (pair). Yellow/green/pink and blue/pink. 6-1/2" tall. With heart bubbles. $85-90 pair. Shell salt & pepper shakers. Pink/blue. $15-18 pair

Lefton's Exclusive, Japan
Mermaids on dolphins (pair), stamped 6445. Light pink & pearl white, jewel eye on dolphins. 6-1/4" long. With bubbles. $160-170 pair. Shell & starfish salt & pepper shakers. $15-18 pair

Freeman-McFarlin Original
Fish wall pockets. Yellow, pink, green & white. 11" long. $65-70 each

Lefton's Japan
Mermaid (#1210). Green tail. 6-1/4" long, 4-1/2" high. $75-80.

Japan
Seahorse (#P302). Green & pink, 6-1/2" tall. $30-34

Shell salt & pepper shaker. $15-18 pair

Atlantic Mold
Mermaid riding dolphin. Pink/green tail, decorated with pearls, shells & jewels, 13" long x 11" high. With bubbles. $140-150

Lefton Exclusive, Japan
Fish marked "3057" (rare). Blue & white, 5-1/2" long; pink & white, 6-1/2" long. With heart bubbles. $110-125 pair.

Norcrest, Japan
Mermaids (pair). Blue/green tail, pink/blue tail, 3-3/4" long. $70-80 pair.

Ink-stamped Japan
Fish. Blue and black. 6-1/2" long. $40-45

DeForest of California
Fish (#6389). Gray and gold, jewel eye. 5-1/2" long. With bubbles. $28-30.

Reddell
Wall pocket with seahorse. Green & white. 7-1/4" tall, 8" wide. $30-$35

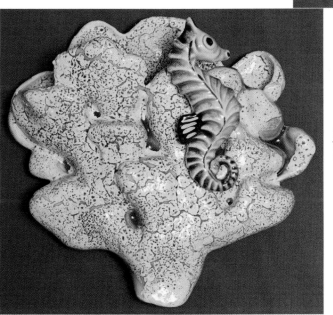

Bradley Exclusive, Japan
Mermaids (set of 3). Green tail. Diving, 3-1/4" long; sitting, 4" long; sleeping, 3-3/4" long. With bubbles. $110-125 set.

Japan
Fish (small red & gold sticker), stamped "JAPAN P-652." Pink & blue, Large, 6" tall; medium, 4-1/2" tall; small, 3-1/2" tall. With bubbles. $70-75 set.

Japan
Fish wall pocket (#1487). Blue & yellow, 7-1/2" long, 6" high. With bubbles. $40-45.

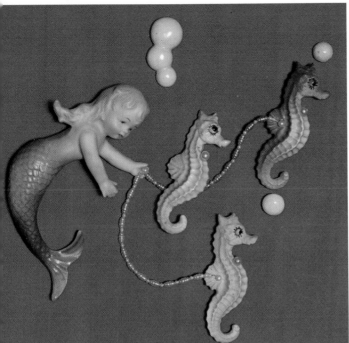

Lefton's Exclusive, Japan
Mermaid with purple tail and 3 blue and purple seahorses (#2223). With bubbles. $125-135 set.

No mark
Fish (set of 3). Bisque, blue/pink/white. All 5-1/2" long. With heart bubbles. $75-80 set

Joty
Mermaids (set of 4). Orange tails, decorated with shells and jewels. Large, 9" tall; with mirror & with harp, 5-1/2"; with arrow, 5-1/4". With bubbles. $160-170 set.

Freeman-McFarlin Originals, El Monte, California
Mermaids (set of 4). Pink & gold tail (also made with green & gold tails). Large, 9" tall; small with bubble, 6" tall; small sleeping, 5-1/2" long; small sitting, 4" tall. With bubbles. $160-170 set.

Freeman-McFarlin Originals, El Monte, California
Large mermaid caddie, 8" tall, $100-125. Soap dish, 7" tall, $75-85. Small mermaid sitting, hand under chin, 5-1/4" tall, $45-50. Small mermaid laying, hand under chin, 5-1/2" long, $45-50. Small mermaid sleeping, 5" long, $45-50.

Freeman-McFarlin Originals, El Monte, California
Same as preceding set with the addition of two small mermaids, one on the bottom & the other on the top left. The additional mermaids are $40-50 each

DeForest of California
Mermaid. Pink & gold tail, 6" long. With bubbles. $70-75.
Fish (set of 3). Pink/brown & gold. Large, 6-1/4" long; small, 4" long. $65-70 set.

Ceramicraft, San Clemente, California
Fish (set of 4). Aqua and black. Large wall pocket, 10" long; medium, 6-1/2" long; small, 5" long; extra-small, 3-1/2" long. With bubbles. $110-125 set.

Norcrest (P-826), Japan
Mermaids (pair). Pink tail, blue tail. 5-1/2" tall. With bubbles. $110-125 pair.

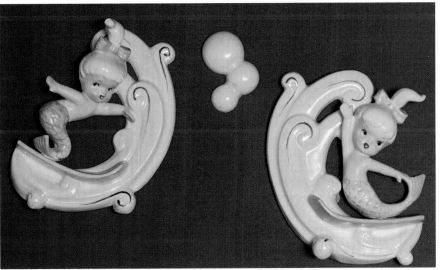

Lefton's Exclusive, Japan
Mermaids (3107). Green tails, red hair. Large, 9" tall; with bubble, 5-1/2"; with mirror, 4-1/4" tall. With bubbles. $155-165 set.

Ceramicraft, San Clemente, California
Fish (set of 6). Pink & black. Large wall pocket, 9-1/2" long; medium-large, 7"; medium, 5-1/2"; medium-small, 5"; small, 4-1/2"; extra small, 3-3/4" long. With bubbles. $120-135 set.

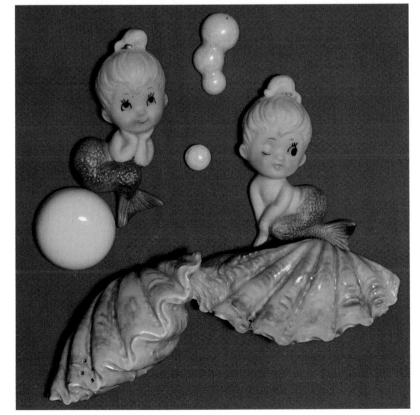

***Top:* Ceramicraft, San Clemente, California**
Fish (set of 3). Yellow/black/white, jewel eyes. 5-3/4"
long. With bubbles. $75-80 set.

***Bottom:* Ink-stamped, Japan**
Fish (pair). Blue/pink/black. Large, 9" long; small, 6-
1/2" long. $38-45 pair.

Bradley Exclusive, Japan
Mermaids sitting on large bubbles (pair).
Green tail. 4" tall. $90-100 pair.
Shell salt & pepper shakers. $25-30 pair.

DeForest of California, Duarte, California
Fish. Black/pink/white/gold, jewel in tail & bubbles.
Large, 6-1/2" long; Medium/small, 4-1/2" long.
With bubbles. $90-95 set.

Tropic Treasures by Ceramicraft, California
Fish. Green & gray. Large, 9-3/4" tall; medium, 5-
1/2", small, 4"; extra-small, 3-1/4". With bubbles.
$70-75 set

Freeman-McFarlin
Fish (pair). Brown & pearl. 8" long, 7-1/2" tall. With heart bubbles.
$110-125 pair.

Py, Japan
Mermaids (pair), left & right. Red tail, green spotted tail, 6-1/4" tall. With bubbles. $110-120 pair.

No Mark, Japan
Mermaid with harp (center). Blue/green tail, 6-1/4" tall. $55-60.

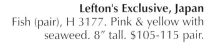

Lefton's Exclusive, Japan
Fish (pair), H 3177. Pink & yellow with seaweed. 8" tall. $105-115 pair.

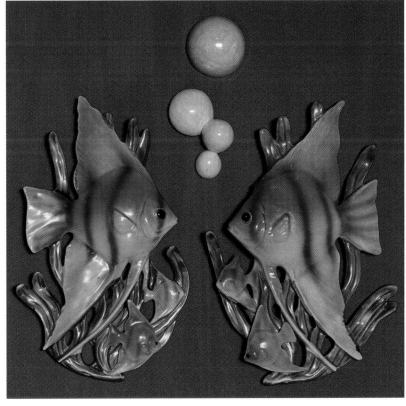

Tropic Treasures by Ceramicraft, San Clemente, California
Fish wall pocket. Purple & black. Large, 8-1/2" long; medium, 5-3/4"; small, 4-1/2"; extra-small, 3" long. With bubbles. $110-125 set.

Ceramicraft, San Clemente, California
Fish (set of 5). Sets are rare & take time to find and put together. Pink and black. Large, 9" long; small, 3-3/4" long. With bubbles. $90-95 set.

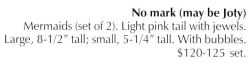

No mark (may be Joty)
Mermaids (set of 2). Light pink tail with jewels. Large, 8-1/2" tall; small, 5-1/4" tall. With bubbles. $120-125 set.

Tropic Treasures by Ceramicraft, San Clemente, California
Fish (set of 5) Pink and black. Large 4-1/2", medium, 4-1/4"; small, 3-1/2"; extra-small, 2-3/4". With gold bubbles. $70 - 75 set.

Ceramicraft, San Clemente, California
Angelfish. Maroon/pink & black.
Large, 12-1/2" high x 10-1/2" long;
medium, 7-1/4" high x 6-1/2" long;
small, 5-1/4" high x 4-1/4" long;
extra-small, 4-1/4" high x 3-1/4"
long. Sets are Rare. $100-110 set.

Bradley, Japan
Mermaid. Pink/gold tail. 5-1/4" tall.
$40-45.

Japan
Fish (set of 5). Blue & yellow, pink &
yellow, 4", 3-1/2", and 2" long. $80-
85 set.

Norcrest, Japan
Mermaid sitting on bubble. Yellow tail.
5" tall. $40-45.

Japan
Fish (set of 6), small blue/white sticker.
Green & white, yellow & white, pink &
blue. Large, 5-1/4" tall; medium,
2-3/4" long; small 2" long. $55-60 set.

DeForest of California, Duarte, California
Fish and fish soapdish. Blue/white/gold. Large, 7-3/4"
long; medium, 3-1/2"; small, 2"; soapdish, 7-3/4";
extra-large, 9-1/2" long. With bubbles. $115-125 set.

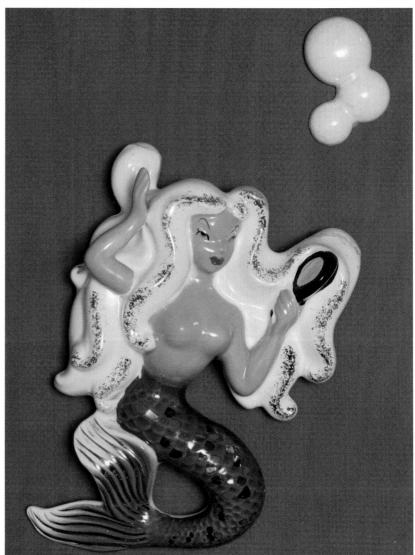

Norcrest China Co., Japan
Mermaid holding mirror (P387). White
hair, green and red tail. 7" tall. $60-65.

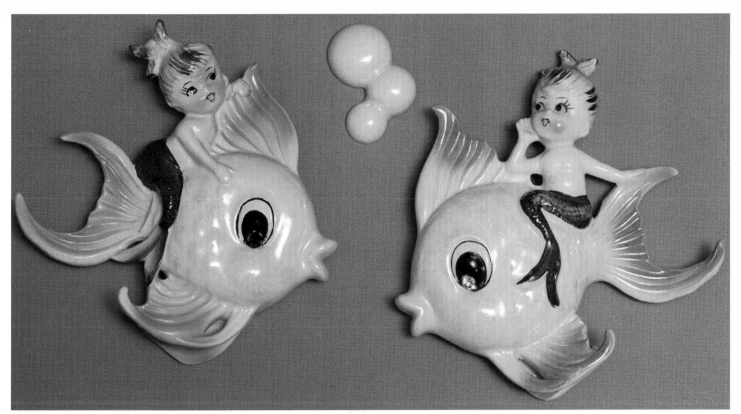

Bradley Exclusives, Japan
Mermaids on fish (pair). Pink & blue, jewel eyes.
6" long. With bubbles. $95-105 pair.

No mark
Mermaids (pair). Pink and gold tails. 5" tall. $60-65 pair.

Bradley Exclusives, Japan
SSeahorses (set of 3). Pink & blue. Large, 6-1/2" high; small, 4" high.
With bubbles. $55-$65 set.
Shell salt & pepper shakers. Pink/blue. $25-30.

Kelvin
Mermaid, 1951 (W 418). Yellow hair, Pink tail. 7" tall. $65-75.

Freeman-McFarlin Original
Fish. Pink & pearl. 2-1/2" long. $22-25.

Pandora Potteries, Santa Monica, California
Fish wall pocket. Pink & blue. 9-1/4" tall x 9-1/2" long. $40-45.

Japan
Mermaids holding fish (pair).
Pink tails. 6-3/4" tall. $90-100
pair.

Japan
Mermaids (pair). Green glitter tails. 5" tall. $90-100 pair.

No mark
Fish (pair). Red & white. 6-1/2" tall.
$60-75 pair.

No mark, Japan
Mermaids holding fish (pair). White/pink with green tails. Right, 4-3/4" tall; left, 5-3/4" tall. $95-100 pair.

Ceramicraft, San Clemente, California
Fish (set of 3). Brown and pearl. Large, 8-3/4"; small, 5-1/2". $50-55 set.

Freeman-McFarlin Originals
Fish, with bubbles. Pink and gold. Large, 9" long. $45-50. Small (pair), 5-1/2" long. $50-55 pair.

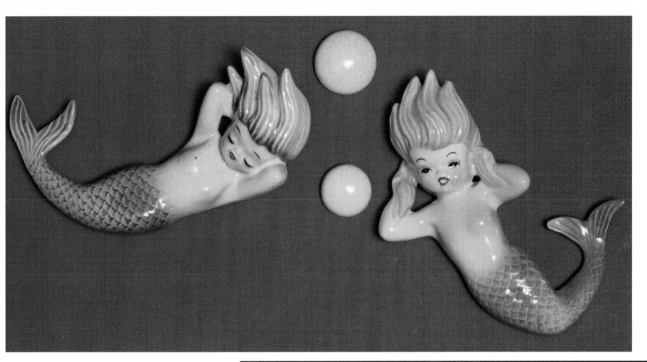

Norcrest, Japan
Mermaids (pair) Blue tail & pink tail. 5-1/2″ tall. With bubbles. $70-75 pair.

Gilner, Japan
Fish wall pockets (set of 3). Yellow/white. Large, 7″ long; small, 5-1/4″ long. $70-75 set.

S. L. Cluter
Mermaid soap dish, 1960. Pink with glitter glass-decorated tail. 9-1/2″ tall. With bubble. $60-75.

Freeman-McFarlin
Fish (set of 2). Black/pink/pearl. Large, 9″
long; small 5-1/2″. $50-60 set.

Semco, Japan
Fish wall pockets (pair), Green/red/yellow. 6-1/2″ long. $50-60 pair.

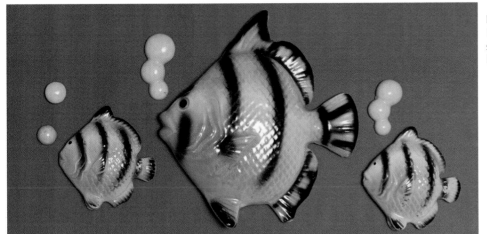

No mark
Fish (set of 3). Blue & yellow with black stripes. Large, 5-1/4" long; small, 2-1/2" long. $22-25 set.

Ceramicraft, San Clemente, California
Fish. Green & black. 4-1/2" long. $15-18.

Japan
Mermaid (marked "#201"). Green tail. 7" long. With bubbles. $50-55.

Norcrest China, Japan
Fish wall pockets. Pink and yellow. 8" long. $35-38 each.

Ceramicraft, San Clemente, California
Fish. Black & gold, jewel eyes. Small fish (set of 3), 6" long, $18-25 each. Two large fish, 12" tall. $38-45 each.

Freeman-McFarlin Originals, El Monte, California
Fish. Large, pink/pearl/black, 12-1/2" tall, 8" long, $70-75.
Fish wall pocket. Medium, pink/pearl/black, 7" tall. $22-25.
Fish. Medium, yellow/brown, black/gold, aqua/black, 7" tall. $12-16 each.
Fish. Small, 3" tall, 1-3/4" long. $8-10 each.

Reddell
Sea fern & fish wall pocket (3 piece set). Fish, 3-1/2" & 3" long. $65-75 set.

No mark
Fish wall pocket. Red and white, 6-1/4"
long. $28-32.

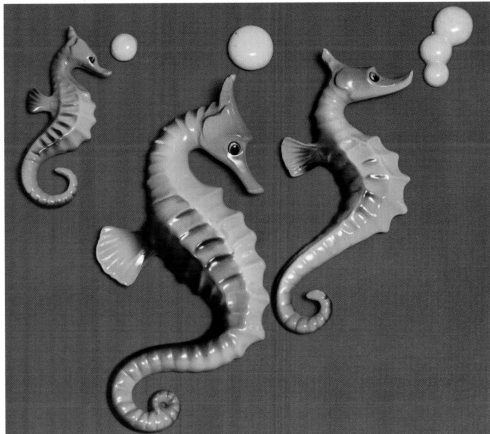

Kelvin Exclusive, Japan
Seahorses (set of 3). Yellow/brown/green. Large, 8-1/2" tall;
medium, 6" tall; small, 4-1/2" tall. $65-70 set.

Napco, Japan
Mermaid wall pocket. Orange & gold tail.
8" tall. With bubbles. $65-75.

No Mark
Fish wall pocket. Yellow & white. 6-3/4" long. With bubbles. $40-45.

Ceramicraft, San Clemente, California
Fish (set of 3). Pink & black, jewel eyes. 5-1/4" long. With bubbles. $85-90 set.

Ceramicraft, San Clemente, California
Mermaid on fish, early. Green tail.
6" long. $25-35.

Norcrest, Japan
Mermaids (pair), marked P-895.
Pink tail, blue tail. 5-1/4" tall.
$80-90 pair.

Ceramicraft, San Clemente, California
Fish wall pocket. Yellow & black. 10" long $36-40.
Fish (set of 3). Mauve & pearl. Medium, 6-1/2" long;
small, 5"; extra-small, 3-1/2" long. $85-90 set.

No mark
Fish (pair). Yellow and pink. Large,
4-1/2" long; small, 2-1/2" long.
$22-$25 pair.

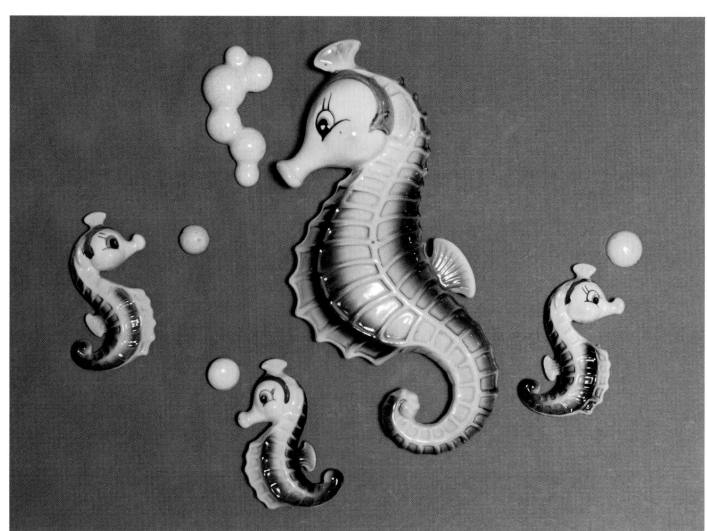

No mark (believed to be Japan)
Seahorses (set of 4) Yellow/blue/pink. Large, 7" tall; small, 2-1/2" tall.
$55-60 set.

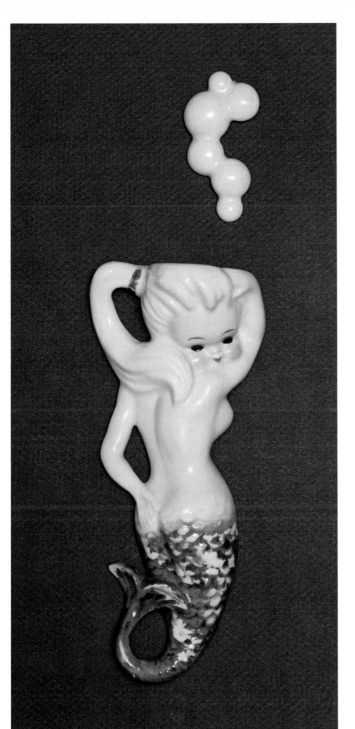

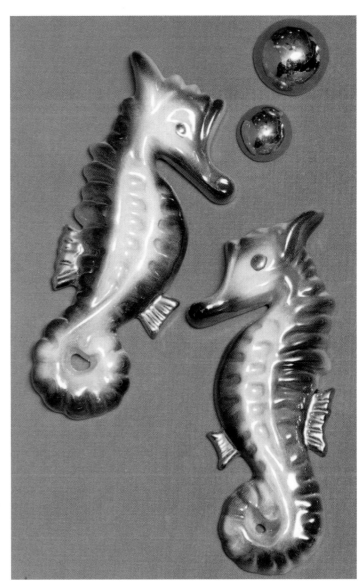

Bradley Exclusive
Mermaid wall pocket. Aqua tail. 6-1/2″ tall. $45-50.

Ceramicraft, San Clemente, California
Seahorses (pair). Green/pearl & gold. 5-1/2″ tall. With bubbles. $36-$40 pair.

Norcrest, Japan
Mermaid surfing. Pink/green tail. 5" tall. $40-45.

Lefton
Seahorse. $25-$30.

Japan
Mermaid with harp. Green tail. 5-1/4" tall. $25-30.

Japan
Mermaids on fish (pair). Green tails. 5-1/2" long. With bubbles. $50-60 pair.

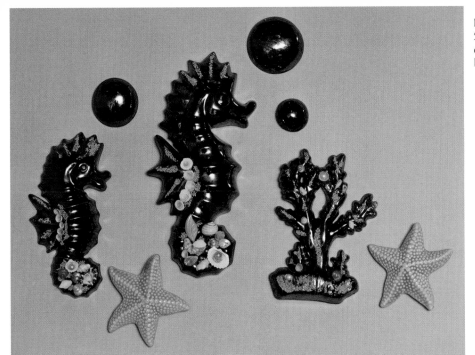

No mark
Seahorse (set of 2) & sea fan. Black, decorated with seashells. With black bubbles. $55-65 set.

No mark
Fish. Red and white. 7-1/4" long, 3-3/4" high. $18-22.

No mark
Fish (pair). Yellow & black. Large, 8" tall; small, 7" tall. $40-45 pair.

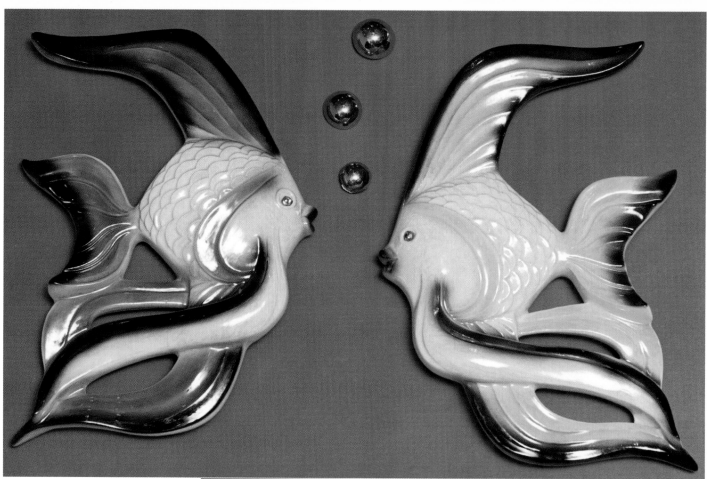

Ceramicraft, San Clemente, California
Fish (pair). Yellow/black/white and blue/black/white, jewel eyes. 8-1/4" long, 12" tall. With bubbles. $90-110 pair.

Nameth Enterprises, Made in Japan
Fish wall pocket. Green & gold. 8-3/4" long. With bubbles. $42-46 pair.

Lefton Exclusive, Japan
Mermaid. Green tail. $75-80.

Japan (Stamped)
Shell wall pocket. White & gold with pink flowers. $20-24.

No mark
Seahorse. Black & gold. 16" tall. With bubbles. $50-60.

Japan
Seahorse. Black/brown/yellow & orange. 6″ tall. $22-25.

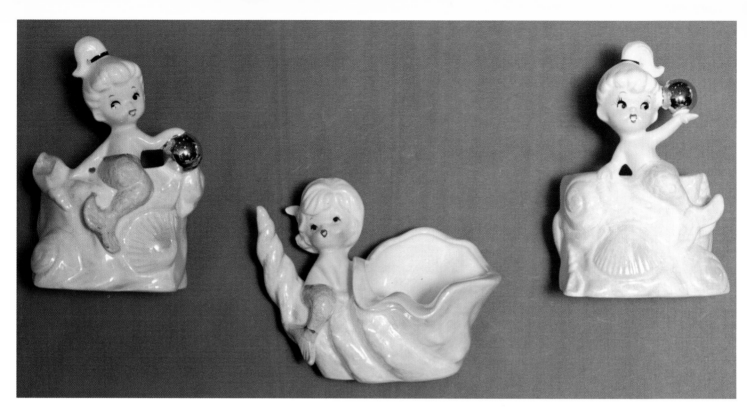

Norcrest
Left to right: Mermaid planters 5950, E-812, and E-950. Blue tail, with gold bubble, 5" high; Blue tail, 4" high; Pink, 5" high. $40-50 each.

Japan (blue & white sticker)
Fish wall pocket. Pink & yellow. 7" long. With bubbles. $28-35.

No mark
Fish planter. Yellow & green. $25-30.

C N C, Los Angeles and Japan
Fish (set of 5). Pink/yellow/white. Large, 6-1/4" high; medium, 2-1/2" high; small, 1-3/4" high. $38-45 set.

Freeman-McFarlin Original
Seahorses (set of 4). Pink &
black. Large, 6-1/2" tall; small, 1-
1/2" tall. $60-65 set.

No mark (Japan)
Mermaids (pair). Bisque, brown glitter
tails. 5" tall. With bubbles. $70-80
pair.

DeForest of California
Fish. Blue, black and white. 9-3/4" long,
11-1/4" high. $38-40.

82

Norcrest, Japan
Mermaid with Seahorse Planter (E-338).
Green tail. 6-1/4" tall. $45-50.

No mark, Japan
Fish (pair). Pink/blue/gold, jewel eyes. 5-1/4"
long. With bubbles. $44-48 pair.

Ceramicraft, San Clemente, California
Fish. Black/gold. Large, 12-1/2" high x 10-1/2"
long; medium, 7-1/4" high x 6-1/2" long;
medium small, 6" high x 5-3/4" long; small, 5-
1/4" high x 4-1/4" long; extra-small, 4-1/4" high
x 3-1/4" long. With bubbles. $105-115 set.

Ceramicraft, San Clemente, California
Fish. Black & gold, jewel eyes. Large, 12-1/2" long, 11-1/4" high, $75-85. Small, 5-1/2" long, $22-24 each.

S.L. Cluter
Mermaid wall-hanging soap dish. 9-1/2" tall. With bubbles. $60-75.

Japan
Mermaids (mini). On turtle, 1-3/4" long, 2" high, green tail. Reclining
mermaid, 2-1/2" long, 1-1/2" high, green/gold tail. $20-25 each.
Mermaid salt & pepper shakers, 3-3/4" tall, green and pink tails.
$80-85 set.

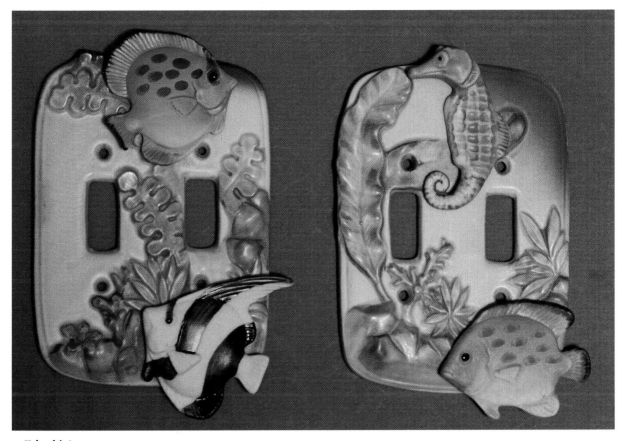

Takashi, Japan
Light switch plate (new) made in several designs, single & double
switches, it makes a complementary decorating addition. Marked
"San Francisco 94103 – Made in Japan."

Row 1 (top, left to right)

1. **Grayson Arts** seahorse. Pink, 8" long. $20-24.
2. **Norcrest, Japan.** Fish wall pocket (#P-327). Dark green & peach. 7" long. $28-34.
3. **Norcrest, Japan.** Fish (group of 3), #P-326. Dark green & peach, 3-3/4", 2-3/4" & 2" long. $12-15 ea.
4. **Ceramicraft.** Fish. Dark pink/black. 8" long. $36-40.

Row 2 (left to right)

1. **Tropic Treasures by Ceramicraft.** Fish. Pink/black. 11-1/2" long. With bubbles. $45-48.
2. **Tropic Treasures by Ceramicraft.** Fish (set of 3). Yellow/Black. Medium, 7", $20-24; small, 4-1/2", $15-18; large wall pocket, 9-1/2", $32-36

Row 3

1. **Freeman-McFarlin Original.** Fish (group of 2). Blue/black. Large, 4-1/2" long x 7" high, $12-16; small, 1-3/4" long x 3" high, $5-8.
2. **No Mark.** Fish (set of 3). Pink/blue/white. Large, 6" long; small, 2 1/3" long. $24-28 set.
3. **Ceramicraft.** Fish. Blue/black. 9" long. $28-32.

Row 4

1. **Ceramicraft.** Fish (set of 4). Black/gold. 6", 5-1/4", 4-1/2", 3-1/4" long. $56-60 set. Note: A large 9-1/2" long wall pocket was made in this style, but is not shown.
2. **DeForest of California.** Fish (set of 2). Pink/white/gold. Large, 8-1/4"; small, 4-1/4". With bubbles. $40-45 set.

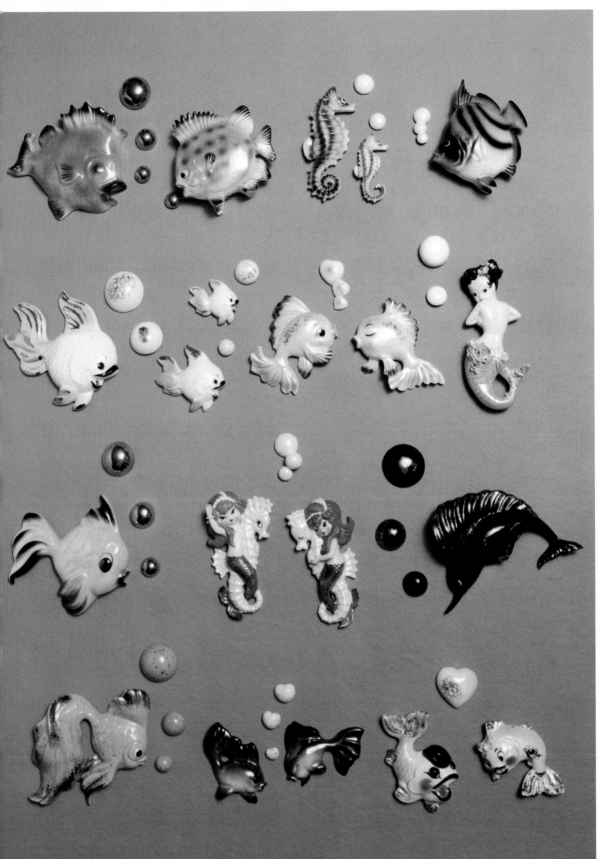

Row 1 (top, left to right)

1. **Tropic Treasures by Ceramicraft.** Fish wall pocket. Pink/black. 7-3/4" long. $28-32.
2. **Japan (Wreath).** Fish wall pocket or freestanding. Pink/blue. $28-32.
3. **Bradley Exclusive Japan.** Seahorses (set of 2). Blue/pink. Large 6-1/2", $20-22; small 4", $12-15.
4. **PY Japan Design Center.** Fish wall pocket & freestanding, marked 9/795. Pink/black. 6" long. $28-32.

Row 2

1. **DeForest of California.** Fish (set of 3). Violet/white/gold. Large, 7-3/4"; medium, 4-3/4"; small, 2". With bubbles. $45-50 set.
2. **No mark.** Fish (pair). Blue/yellow, 5-1/2" long; pink/yellow, 6" long. With heart bubbles. $38-42 pair.
3. **Rose.** Mermaid, 1958. Aqua tail. Pink sea shells and jewels. 8-1/2" tall. $60-65.

Row 3

1. **Tropic Treasures by Ceramicraft.** Fish. Yellow/black. 7-1/2". $24-28.
2. **Lefton.** Mermaids on seahorses (pair) marked 3158 Japan. Red hair, green tail, white seahorse. Each 7-1/4" high. $180-190 pair.
3. **Freeman-McFarlin Original.** Fish wall pocket. Black/gold. 8-1/2". With bubbles. $26-30.

Row 4

1. **Freeman-McFarlin Original.** Fish. Powder blue & gold. 9" long. With bubbles. $35-40.
2. **Freeman-McFarlin Original.** Fish (pair). Green. 5" long. With bubbles. $22-26 pair.
3. **DeForest of California.** Fish (pair). Violet/white/black/gold, 5-3/4". With heart bubble. $38-45 pair.

Row 1 (Top, left to right)

1. **Ceramicraft, San Clemente, California.** Fish wall pocket. Yellow & black. 9-1/2" long. With bubbles. $45-48.
2. **Nepco, Japan.** Mermaid wall pocket. Aqua tail. 8" tall. With bubbles. $65-75.
3. **Ceramicraft, San Clemente, California.** Seahorse. Aqua & gold. 4-1/2" tall. $8-10.
4. **Ceramicraft, San Clemente, California.** Fish wall pocket. Pink & black, 10" long. $36-40.

Row 2

1. **No mark.** Fish. Light brown & pearl. 8-1/2" tall. $18-22.
2. **Ceramicraft, San Clemente, California.** Fish (set of 3). Mauve & pearl. Large, 6-1/2" long; medium, 5"; small, 3-1/2". With bubbles. $46-50 set.
3. **Lefton.** Fish, marked 60114. White/black/gold. 6-1/2" long. $14-18.

Row 3

1. **Tropic Treasures by Ceramicraft.** Fish wall pocket. Yellow & white. 7-3/4" long. $28-32.
2. **Bradley Exclusive, Japan.** Seahorses (set of 2). Pink & white, 4" tall. With bubbles. $12-16 ea.
3. **Kelvin.** Mermaid, marked 1951W418. Pink tail. 7" tall. $65-70.
4. **Tropic Treasures by Ceramicraft.** Fish (pair). Yellow & black. Large, 7-1/2" long; small, 4-1/2" long. With bubbles. $40-45 pair.

Row 4

1. **Tropic Treasures by Ceramicraft.** Fish wall pocket. Black & gold. 10-1/2" long. $36-40.
2. **Ceramicraft, San Clemente, California.** Fish (two). Black & gold. 3-3/4" long. $12-16 ea.
3. **Freeman-McFarlin Original.** Fish (set of 2). White & gold. 2-3/4" long. With bubbles. $10-14 ea.
4. **Nameth Enterprises, California.** Fish wall pockets (pair). Purple & gold. 8-3/4" long. With bubbles. $36-42 pair.

Row 1 (top, left to right)

1. **Tropic Treasures by Ceramicraft.** Fish. Aqua & black. 11-1/2" long. With bubbles $45-48

2. **Tropic Treasures by Ceramicraft.** Fish. Yellow & black. These are the babies for #1, except for color. I hope to find them in aqua. 3-3/4" & 2" long. $12-16 ea.

3. **Marroco-Decor, Made in Japan.** Fish wall pockets (pair). Dark green/yellow/gold. 6" long. $22-25 ea.

Row 2

1. **Stamped Japan.** Fish. Pink/green/yellow with dark stripes. 6-1/2" tall. $22-25.

2. **Stamped Japan.** Mermaids holding gold starfish (pair). Green tails. 6-1/2" tall, 4-1/2" long. $175-$190 pair.

3. **No mark.** Seahorses (pair) wall pockets. Purple & gold, 8-1/2" tall. With bubbles. $42-50 pair.

Row 3

1. **Ceramicraft, San Clemente, California.** Fish. Aqua and black. 7-1/4" tall. $26-30.

2. **Ceramicraft, San Clemente, California.** Fish. Green and black. 3-3/4" long. (Matches #1 in different color). $12-15.

3. **No mark.** Seahorses (set of 2). Yellow/blue/pink. Large, 7" tall; small, 2-1/2" tall. Believed to be Japan. $35-40 set.

4. **Josef Originals, Monrovia, California/Japan.** Fish. Powder blue & gold. 7-3/4" long. $50-55.

Row 4

1. **Bradley Exclusive, Japan.** Fish wall pockets (set of 2). Yellow/pink/blue/gold and blue/pearl & gold. 6" long. $22-25 ea.

2. **Reddell.** Fish (set of 3). Pink & white and green & white. 4" long. $15-18 ea.

3. **Freeman-McFarlin Original.** Fish wall pocket (rare). Yellow/orange. 11" long. $65-70.

Row 1 (top, left to right)

1. Tropic Treasures by Ceramicraft. Fish wall pocket. Blue/white. 9" long, With bubbles. $26-30

2. No mark. Mermaid. Pink with blue/green tail. 6-1/4" long. $55-60.

3. PY Japan Design Center. Mermaid. Pink with green tail, 6 1/4" long. $55-60.

4. Tropic Treasures by Ceramicraft. Fish wall pocket. Lime green/black. 9-1/2" long. With bubbles. $35-40.

Row 2

1. DeForest of California. Fish (set of 3) marked 1956 USA. Deep bright pink, Large, 7-3/4"; medium, 4-3/4"; small, 2". With bubbles. $50-55 set.

2. DeForest of California. Seahorse. Deep pink. 7-3/4" long. $18-22.

3. No mark. Fish. Yellow with narrow green & orange stripes. $16-18.

Row 3

1. Freeman-McFarlin. Mermaids (set of 2). Dark green tails. Large, 9", $65-70; small, 5-1/2". $40-45.

2. Ceramicraft. Fish. Turquoise with black stripes. 12-1/2" high by 10-1/2" long. With bubbles. $44-48.

3. No mark. Seahorses (set of 2). Maroon/black. 8" & 4-1/2". With bubbles. $55-60 set

Row 4

1. Josef Originals, Monrovia, California/ Japan. Fish. Pink/black. 6-1/2" long. $35-40

2. Irene Smith. Fish, Black/gold, 7-1/2" long. $16-18.

3. Ceramicraft. Fish (set of 3). Green/black. Small, 3"; medium, 4-1/2"; large, 5-3/4" long. With bubbles. $60-65 set.

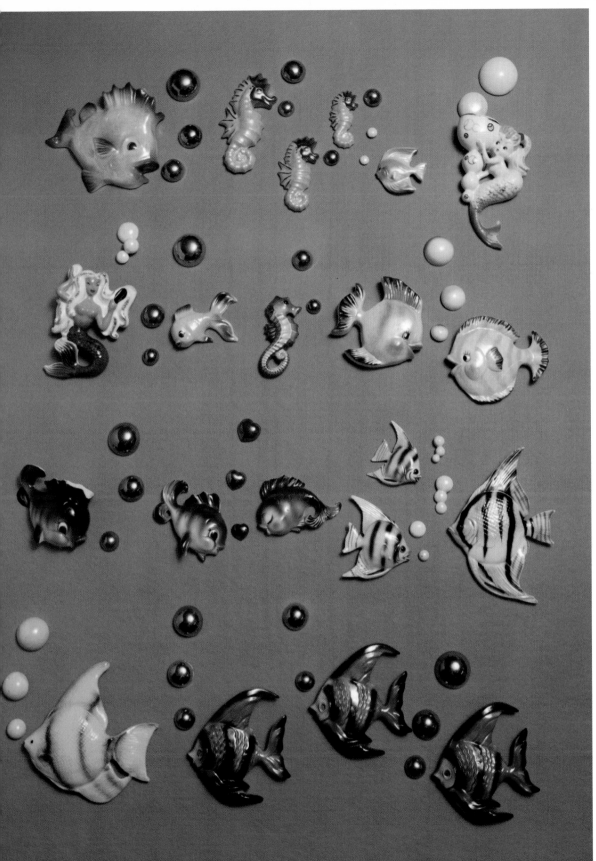

Row 1 (top, left to right)

1. **Tropic Treasures by Ceramicraft.** Fish wall pocket. Green & brown, 7-3/4" long. $28-32
2. **No Mark.** Seahorses (set of 3) Aqua & gold, Large, 7" tall; medium, 5" tall; small, 4" tall. $30-35 set.
3. **Freeman-McFarlin.** Fish (rare). Purple/pearl/gold. 3" long. $22-24.
4. **Napco, Japan.** Mermaid wall pocket. Orange & gold tail. 8" tall. With bubbles. $65-75.

Row 2

1. **Norcrest China Co., Japan.** Mermaid wall pocket, marked P387. Green tail with red & gold markings. 7" tall. $60-65.
2. **Ceramicraft, San Clemente, California.** Fish. Yellow & gray. 4" long. $15-18.
3. **Bradley Exclusive, Japan.** Seahorse. Aqua/blue/gold. 5" tall. $16-20.
4. **Bradley Exclusive, Japan.** Fish (pair). Green/pearl/gold and Yellow/pearl/gold. 6" long. $22-25 ea.

Row 3

1. **Norcrest, Japan.** Fish wall pocket, marked P 406. Emerald green. 5-3/4" long. $28-30
2. **Norcrest Japan.** Fish (pair), marked P 395. Emerald green. 5" long. $40-45 pair.
3. **Semco.** Fish (set of 2). Blue/pink/black. Large, 4-1/4" tall; small, 3-1/2" tall. $30-35 set
4. **UCAGO, United China & Glass Co. Inc., Japan.** Fish, unusually fine quality. Blue/pink/yellow with black stripes. 9" tall. $70-75.

Row 4

1. **Pandora Potteries, Santa Monica, California.** Fish. Yellow with green stripes. 7-1/2" tall. With bubbles. $25-28.
2. **Ceramicraft, San Clemente, California.** Fish (set of 3). Burgundy & black, jewel eyes. 6" long. $22-25 ea.

Row 1 (top, left to right)

1. Tropic Treasures by Ceramicraft. Fish wall pocket. Pink & black. 9-1/2" long. With bubbles. $45-48.

2. Bradley Exclusive, Japan. Mermaid on fish wall pocket. Pink & white, jewel eye on fish, green tail on mermaid. 6" long. $45-50.

3. Ceramicraft San Clemente, California. Fish (pair). Pink & gray. 7" long. With bubbles. $36-42 pair.

Row 2

1. Marroco Decor Made in Japan. Girl fish wall pocket. Yellow & brown. 6" long. $20-24.

2. Bradley Exclusive, Japan. Boy fish wall pocket. Yellow & brown. 6" long. $20-24 ea.

3. Ceramicraft, San Clemente, California. Fish (set of 3). Brown & white, jewel eyes. 6" long. $18-25 ea.

Row 3

1. Tropic Treasures by Ceramicraft. Fish wall pocket. Green & pearl white. 7-3/4" long. With bubbles. $28-32

2. McFarlin Potteries. Seahorse. Pink & black. 6-1/2" tall. $22-28

3. Ceramicraft, San Clemente, California. Fish (set of 3). Aqua/black/white, jewel eyes, 6" long. $18-23 ea.

Row 4

1. Tropic Treasures by Ceramicraft. Fish wall pocket. Pink and black. 10-1/2" long. $36-40

2. No Mark. Fish (group of 4). Black & gold. One large, 6" high, $14-16; three small, 4" high, $8-12 ea.

3. No Mark. Mermaids (set of 2). Light pink tail with jewels. Large, 8-1/2" tall; small, 5-1/4" tall. With jeweled bubbles. $120-$125 set.

Row 1 (top, left to right)

1. **Japan.** Fish (set of 2), marked 7322. Pink/blue/yellow/white, 6-1/2", 8". With bubbles. $36-40 pair.
2. **Bradley Exclusive, Japan.** Fish double wall pocket. Pink. 6-1/2". $20-25
3. **Tropic Treasures by Ceramicraft.** Fish wall pocket. Aqua/black. 10" long. $36-40

Row 2

1. **No mark.** Fish (set of 3). Yellow/white/gold. Large, 6"; medium, 4-1/2"; small, 3". With bubbles. $24-30 set.
2. **DeForest of California.** Fish (set of 3). Violet/white/gold. Large, 8-1/4"; small, 4". With bubbles. $70-75 set.

Row 3

1. **Norcrest, Japan.** Fish wall pocket, #327. Dark green/pink. 7" long. $28-34.
2. **No mark.** Fish. Green/yellow. 6" long. $10-15.
3. **No mark, believed to be Japan.** Fish. Pink with black stripes. 4-1/2" long. $15-18.
4. **Freeman-McFarlin Original.** Fish wall pocket (rare). Green. 11" long. $65-70.

Row 4

1. **Stamped "Made in Japan."** Fish wall pocket. Yellow with black stripes, 7" high. $14-16.
2. **NAPCO, Japan.** Fish (set of 5). Black/green/white. Lady, 6" high; man, 6-1/2" high; babies, 2-1/2" high. $80-85 set.
3. **CNC, Los Angeles/Japan.** Seahorses (pair). Pink/white. 5" long. $12-15 ea.
4. **Tropic Treasures by Ceramicraft.** Fish wall pocket. Mauve/white. 7-3/4" long. $28-32.

93

Row 1 (top, left to right)

DeForest of California. Fish (group of 5). Rose brown/white/gold. Soap dish (far left), 7-3/4" long, $20-24; large, 7-3/4" long, with bubbles, $25-30; medium, 3-1/2" long, $15-18; small, 2" long, $8-10; extra large, 9-1/2" long, $36-40. Complete set, with bubbles, $115-125.

Row 2

1. **No mark.** Fish (two). Blue & brown. 5-1/4" long. $12-15 ea.
2. **Japan.** Fish (group of 5). Black & gold. Two small, 4" long, $5-8; two medium, 5-3/4" long, $8-10; large, 8" long, with small blue & white sticker, $10-15.

Row 3

1. **No mark.** Fish wall pocket. Green/brown/gold. 5" long. $18-22.
2. **Freeman-McFarlin Original.** Fish kissing (pair). Pink/black/pearl. 5" long. With heart bubbles. $22-26 pair.
3. **Lefton, Japan.** Mermaids (pair). Green tails. 8" tall. $180-190 pair.
4. **No mark.** Fish wall pocket & freestanding. Green/black/pink. 7" tall. $25-30.

Row 4

1. **Tropic Treasures by Ceramicraft.** Fish. Bright green & black. 7-1/2" long. $24-28.
2. **Ceramicraft, San Clemente, California.** Fish. Aqua & black. 4-1/2" long. $8-12.
3. **DeForest of California.** Fish (set of 3). Brown/white/gold, jewels on tail. Large, 6-1/2" long; small, 4-1/4" long. With bubbles. $90-95 set.
4. **No mark.** Mermaid. Yellow & gold tail, 8-1/2" tall. $35-40.

94

Row 1 (top, left to right)

1. **Ceramicraf, San Clemente, California.** Fish. Yellow & black stripes. 12-1/2" high, 10-1/2" long. With bubbles. $44-48.
2. **Lefton's Exclusive, Japan.** Fish. Black & gold. 4-1/4" long. $8-10.
3. **Tropic Treasures by Ceramicraft.** Fish (set of 3). Pink & black. Large, 7-1/2" long; small, 4-1/2". $55-60 set.

Row 2

1. **Bradley Exclusive, Japan.** Fish double wall pocket. Green/yellow/deep pink/gold. 6-1/2" long. $22-25.
2. **No mark.** Mermaids (set of 2). Light yellow, pearl tail, shells & jewels. Large, 9" tall; small, 5-1/2" tall. $110-115 set.
3. **No mark.** Seahorse wall pockets (pair). Yellow & gold. 8-1/2" tall. $42-50 pair.

Row 3

1. **Enesco, Japan.** Fish, seahorse, and starfish (set of 4). Green & pink fish, blue/yellow/pink fish, red starfish, green & blue seahorse. All about 4-1/2". $18-24 set.
2. **No mark.** Fish. Yellow & gold. 5" long. $8-10.
3. **DeForest of California.** Fish (set of 3). Deep pink and gold, with jewels on tail and fins. Large, 6-1/2" long; small, 4-1/4". With bubbles. $90-95 set.

Row 4

1. **No mark.** Fish wall pocket & freestanding. Green/pink/white. 7-1/2" tall. $15-20.
2. **Japan sticker.** Mermaid with eye lashes. Dark green tail. 6-3/4" tall. With bubbles. $45-50.
3. **Ceramicraft, San Clemente, California.** Fish (pair). Black & gold. 7 1/2" tall. With gold heart bubble. $36-42 pair.

Row 1 (top, left to right)

1. **Tropic Treasures by Ceramicraft.** Fish wall pocket. Aqua and black. 9-1/2" long. With bubbles. $40-45.
2. **No mark.** Fish (set of 3). Brown & white, jewel eyes. 5" long. $16-20 ea.
3. **DeForest of California.** Mermaid. Yellow & gold tail. 3" long. $40-45.
4. **No mark.** Fish wall pocket. Pink & gold, 8" long. With four bubbles. $22-25.

Row 2

1. **Lefton, Japan.** Fish wall pockets & freestanding, #216 (pair). Bright pink/yellow/black. 7" long. With bubbles. $58-65 pair.
2. **Norcrest (p639), Japan.** Mermaid with fish. Blue tail. 5-1/2" tall. With bubbles. $75-80.
3. **Bradley Exclusive, Japan.** Fish wall pocket (pair). Yellow/white/gold. 6" long. With bubbles. $38-46 pair.

Row 3

1. **Ceramicraft, San Clemente, California.** Fish (two). Aqua and black. 3" long. $8-10 ea.
2. **Joty.** Mermaids (set of 3). Gold tail, with sea shells & jewels. Large, 8-1/2" tall; medium, 5-1/2" tall; small, 5-1/4" tall. Mold mark. $140-$145 set.
3. **Ceramicraft, San Clemente, California.** Fish, (two). Pink & black. Medium, 5" long, $10-15; small, 3" long, $8-10.

Row 4

1. **Bradley Exclusive, Japan.** Fish wall pockets (set of 4). Green/yellow/gold. 6" long. $22-25 ea.
2. **Ceramicraft, San Clemente, California.** Seahorses (pair). Green/black/gold. 4-1/2" high. $16-20 pair.

Row 1 (Top, left to right)

1. **Tropic Treasures by Ceramicraft.** Fish. Green/black. 7-1/2" long. $24-28.
2. **No mark.** Fish. Yellow/orange with wide green stripes. 6-3/4" long. $16-18.
3. **No mark.** Mermaids (set of 3). Mottled pink tail. Large, 8-3/4" long; medium, 7-1/2" long; small, 4-1/4" long. $75-80 set.

Row 2

1. **CNC, Japan.** Fish (set of 4). Pink/yellow & blue/yellow. Large, 6"; medium, 3"; small, 2". With bubbles. $28-32 set.
2. **No mark.** Fish (set of 3). Pink/white/gold. Large, 6" long; medium, 4-1/2"; small, 3". With bubbles. $24-30 set.
3. **DeForest of California.** Seahorses (set of 3). Yellow/white/gold. Large, 7-3/4" long; small, 4" long. $52-55 set.

Row 3

1. **Bradley Exclusive, Japan.** Fish double wall pocket. Pink/yellow/gold. 6-1/2" long. With bubbles. $22-25.
2. **Freeman-McFarlin Original.** Fish kissing (pair). White & gold. 5" long. With heart bubbles. $28-32 pair.
3. **No mark.** Fish wall pocket. Green/light brown/gold, 6" long. $20-22.
4. **PY, Japan.** Mermaids (pair). Hot pink & yellow tail, green & pink tail. 6-1/4" long. With bubbles. $110-120 pair.

Row 4

1. **Ceramicraft.** Fish. Pink & black, jewel eye. 6" long. $18-25.
2. **Japan.** Mermaids on fish (pair), marked P697. Light blue tails, jewel eyes in fish. 6" long. With bubbles. $80-85 pair.
3. **Ceramicraft.** Fish (pair). Blue/yellow/white. 7" long. With heart bubble. $36-42 pair.

Row 1 (top, left to right)

1. **Tropic Treasures by Ceramicraft.** Fish wall pocket. Aqua & black. 10-1/2" long. $36-40.
2. **No mark.** Mermaid wall pocket. Aqua tail. 6-1/2" tall. $45-50.
3. **Ceramicraft, San Clemente, California.** Fish (set of 2). Black and gold. Small, 5" long. $12-16; large, 9" long, $28-32.

Row 2

1. **Tropic Treasures by Ceramicraft.** Fish wall pocket. Yellow & Black, 7-3/4" long. $28-32
2. **Marroco-Decor, Made in Japan.** Fish wall pockets (pair). Yellow/ light brown/gold. 6" long. With bubbles. $42-46 pair.
3. **Tropic Treasures by Ceramicraft.** Fish. Aqua & black. 7-1/2" long. $24-28.

Row 3

1. **Ceramicraft, San Clemente, California.** Fish (pair). Pink & black, jewel eyes. 6" long. $18-23 ea.
2. **No mark.** Mermaid. Green tail. 5-1/2" tall. $30-35.
3. **Nameth Enterprises, California.** Fish wall pockets (pair). Pink pearl & gold. 8-1/3" long. With bubbles. $36-42 pair.

Row 4

1. **Ceramicraft, San Clemente, California.** Fish. Brown & cream. 12-1/2" long. With bubbles. $44-48.
2. **No mark.** Fish (pair). Light blue & pearl, jewel eyes. 6" long. With bubbles. $30-36 pair.
3. **Ceramicraft, San Clemente, California.** Fish wall pocket. Black and gold. 10" long. With bubbles. $36-40.

Row 1 (top, left to right)

1. **No mark.** Fish wall pocket. Blue/yellow/gold, 5" long. $18-22.
2. **Ceramicraft, San Clemente, California.** Fish (pair). Pink & black. 7-1/2" tall. With bubbles. $36-42 pair.
3. **No mark.** Mermaids (pair). Blue tails, pink sea shells. Large, 9" tall; small, 5-1/2" tall. $85-90 pair.

Row 2

1. **Tropic Treasures by Ceramicraft.** Fish wall pocket. Pink & black. 9" long. $26-30.
2. **No mark.** Fish. Black & gold. 5-3/4" long. $6-8.
3. **No mark.** Fish. Yellow & black, jewel eye. 5-1/2" long. $15-18.
4. **Freeman-McFarlin Original.** Sailfish wall pocket. Green & pink. 9" long. With bubbles. $30-35.

Row 3

1. **DeForest of California.** Mermaids (pair) & seahorses (pair). Purple & gold. Large mermaid, 6" long; small mermaid, 3" long, $115-$125 set. Seahorses. 4" tall. $18-22 ea.
2. **PY Japan, Design Center.** Fish (pair). Cerise & green, jewel eye, 6-1/2" long; blue & cerise, jewel eye, 7" long. $95-100 pair.
3. **PY Japan.** Fish wall pocket & freestanding, marked 9/797. Peach/green/brown. 6-1/2" long. With bubbles. $40-45.

Row 4

1. **Bradley Exclusive.** Mermaids, Wall Pockets (set of 3) Blue tail, Green tail, Red tail, 4" high - $40-45 ea.
2. **Japan.** Mermaids (pair) with small red & gold sticker reading "Japan 11574 & 11576." Green tails. Large, 4-1/2" long; small, 4" long. $115-$125 pair.
3. **Norcrest, Japan.** Fish wall pocket & freestanding, marked P-327. Brown/pink/yellow. 6-1/2" long. $30-35.

Row 1 (top, left to right)

1. **Tropic Treasures by Ceramicraft.** Fish. Royal blue & pearl. 9-1/2" long. $32-36.
2. **Tropic Treasures by Ceramicraft.** Fish. Deep yellow & black. 9-1/2" long. $32-36.
3. **Ceramicraft, San Clemente, California.** Fish. Aqua & black. 9-1/2" long. $35-40.

Row 2

1. **Tropic Treasures by Ceramicraft.** Fish. Aqua & light brown. 9-1/2" long. $32-38.
2. **Tropic Treasures by Ceramicraft.** Fish. Mauve & pearl. 9-1/2" long. $35-40.
3. **Ceramicraft, San Clemente, California.** Fish. Black & gold. 9-1/2" long. $35-40.

Row 3

1. **Tropic Treasures by Ceramicraft.** Fish. Lime green & black. 9-1/2" long. $35-40
2. **Tropic Treasures by Ceramicraft.** Fish. Yellow & light brown. 9-1/2" long. $32-35
3. **Tropic Treasures by Ceramicraft.** Fish. Purple & black. 9-1/2" long. $35-40

Row 4

1. **Tropic Treasures by Ceramicraft.** Fish. Peach & black. 9-1/2" long. $32-35
2. **Tropic Treasures by Ceramicraft.** Fish. Pink & blue. 9-1/2" long. $32-35
3. **Tropic Treasures by Ceramicraft.** Fish. Green & pearl. 9-1/2" long. $32-35

Note: As you see, Ceramicraft made this fish in a variety of colors. You will find that many of the fish and mermaids pictured in this book were also made in different colors.

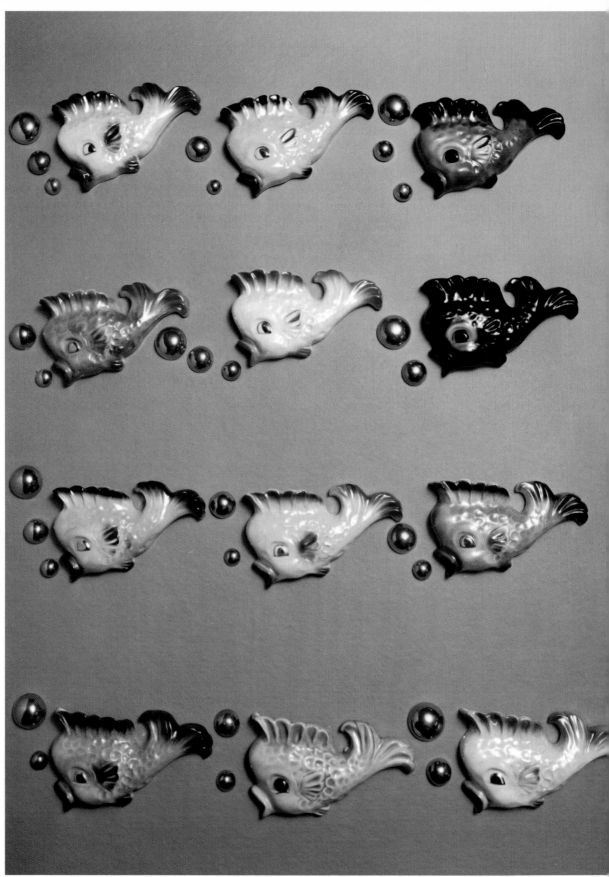

Row 1 (top, left to right)

1. **No mark, believed to be Grayson Arts, California.** Fish (set of 3). Yellow & gold. Large, 6" long; medium, 5-1/2"; small, 3-1/4". $18-20 set.
2. **No mark.** Fish (pair). White, jewel eyes. 6-1/2" tall. $18-20 pair.
3. **No mark, believed to be Ceramicraft, San Clemente, California.** Fish wall pocket. Aqua & pearl. 9-1/4". $28-32

Row 2

1. **Lefton's Exclusive, Japan.** Fish, marked #155B. Black/white/gold. 6" long. $18-23.
2. **Lefton's Exclusive, Japan.** Mermaid & shells, marked 1946. Green tail. Large shell with mermaid, 6" tall; small shells, 1-1/2" wide. $50-55.
3. **Grayson Arts, California.** Fish (pair + 1), pair marked 456, single no number. Turquoise. Each 7" long. $18-20 pair; $10-12 single.

Row 3

1. **Lefton's Exclusive, Japan.** Fish. White & gold. 6-1/4" long. $18-23.
2. **No mark, believed to be Japan.** Mermaid holding fish. Blue tail. 6-3/4" tall. $45-50.
3. **Stamped Japan.** Seahorse. White & gold, jewel eye. 4-1/2" tall. $12-16.
4. **Stamped Japan.** Fish wall pocket. Yellow/white/green. 5-1/2" long . $14-17.
5. **Bradley Exclusive, Japan.** Fish (set of 2). Pink with dark stripes. Large, 5" tall; small, 4" tall. $16-20 set.

Row 4

1. **DeForest, California.** Fish, soapdish & ashtray (set of 2). Black/white/gold. Soapdish, 8" long; ashtray, 7-3/4" long. $20-24 ea.
2. **DeForest, California**. Fish (set of 2). Black/white/gold. Extra large, 9-1/2" long, with bubbles, $36-40; large $25-30.
3. **DeForest, California.** Mermaids (set of 2). Black & gold tail, Large, 6" long; small, 3" long. $115-125 set.

Row 1 (top, left to right)

1. **Tropic Treasures by Ceramicraft.** Fish (this has a silver & black sticker, the only one I have seen to this time). Burgundy & gold. 7-1/2" long. With bubbles. $26-30.

2. **Stamped E-2163, thought to be Japan.** Mermaids with umbrella (pair). Pearl white tails. 5" tall. $85-95 pair.

3. **No mark.** Fish wall pocket. Blue & white. 9-1/2" long. $18-22

Row 2

1. **Freeman-McFarlin Original.** Fish kissing (pair). Pink & gold. 5" long. With heart bubbles. $38-40 set.

2. **Bradley Exclusives, Japan.** Mermaids. Green tails. 4" tall. With heart bubbles. $35-40 ea.

3. **DeForest, California.** Fish (set of 3). Black/white/pink, with jewels on tail. Large, 6-1/2" long; small, 4-1/4" long. With bubbles. $90-95 set.

Row 3

1. **Ceramicraft.** Fish (set of 3). Black & gold, jewel eyes. 6" long. $18-25 ea.

2. **No mark.** Fish (pair). White & gold. 4-1/2" long. With bubbles. $26-30 pair.

Row 4

1. **Bradley Exclusive, Japan.** Seahorses (set of 3). Blue/pink/black. Large, 6-1/2"; small, 4". With bubbles. $35-40 set.

2. **No mark.** Fish. Black & gold. 4-3/4" long. $12-16.

3. **Enesco Imports, Japan.** Fish (set of 4). Pink & blue with burgundy stripes. Large, 6" long, $22-25; small, 3-1/4" long, $12-15.

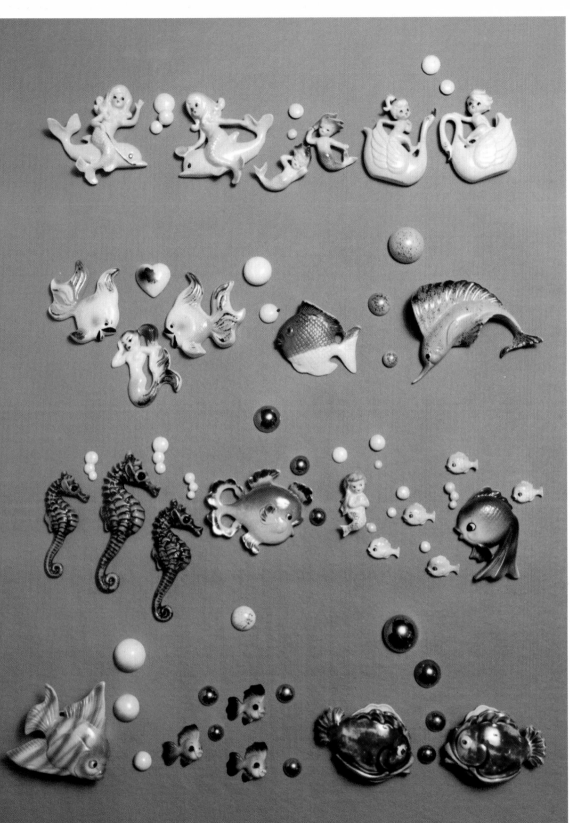

Row 1 (top, left to right)

1. **Japan.** Mermaids on dolphins (pair), small blue & white sticker, stamped 6445. Light pink & pearl white, jewel eye on dolphins. 6-1/4" long. With bubbles. $160-170 pair.

2. **Norcrest Fine China, Japan.** Mermaids (pair) Pink & Blue tail and Blue & Green tail, 3-1/2" tall - $35-40 ea.

3. **Norcrest, Japan.** Mermaids on swans (pair), marked P978. Pink tail & blue tail. 5-1/2" high. $110-120 pair.

Row 2

1. **DeForest.** Fish (pair). Blue /white/gold. 5-1/2" long. With heart bubble. $25-30 pair.
No mark. Mermaid. Blue/white/gold. 5" tall. $30-35.

2. **Stamped Japan.** Fish wall pocket. Brown & white, 5-1/4" long. $12-16.

3. **Freeman-McFarlin Original.** Sailfish wall pocket. Green & gold, 8-1/2" long. With bubbles. $26-30.

Row 3

1. **No mark.** Seahorses (set of 3). Brown. Large, 8-1/2" tall; medium, 7" tall; small, 6-1/2" tall. With bubbles. $45-50 set.

2. **Bradley Exclusives, Japan.** Fish double wall pocket. Yellow/cerise/gold. 6-1/2" long. $22-25.

3. **Norcrest, Japan.** Mermaid. White & gold tail. 3-1/4" tall. $30-35.

4. **Japan.** Fish (set of 6) with small blue & white sticker. One large green & pink, 5-1/4" tall, and 5 small pink & yellow, 2" long. With bubbles. $30-35 set.

Row 4

1. **No mark.** Fish wall pocket/planter. Pink and white. 7-1/2" tall. $22-25.

2. **Freeman-McFarlin Original.** Fish (three). Pink and green. 2-3/4" long. $15-18 ea.

3. **No mark.** Fish wall pockets or freestanding (pair). Maroon/gold/brown. 6" long. $44-50 pair.

Row 1 (top, left to right)

1. **Ceramicraft, San Clemente, California.** Fish (three). Yellow & black and pink & black. 3-3/4" long. $18-20 ea.
2. **Norcrest, Japan.** Mermaid in shell, marked P-35. Silver & white tail. 6-1/2" high. $55-60
3. **Freeman-McFarlin Original.** Fish. Black & gold. 7" high, 4-1/2" long. $12-16.
4. **Ceramicraft, San Clemente, California.** Fish. Pink & black. 9" long. With bubbles. $28-32.

Row 2

1. **No mark.** Fish wall pockets (set of 2). Pink & black, Large, 7" long; small, 4-1/2" long. $24-28 set.
2. **Tropic Treasures by Ceramicraft.** Fish (set of 4). Green & black, large, 7-1/2" long; small, 4-1/2" long. With bubbles. $85-90 set.

Row 3

1. **No mark.** Fish wall pocket and freestanding. Blue/white/gold. 9" tall. $15-20.
2. **No mark.** Fish wall pocket. Maroon/black/gold. 5" long. $20-25.
3. **Lefton.** Fish (set of 3). Black & gold. Large, 5" long; small, 2-1/2" long. With gold heart bubbles. $20-23 set.
4. **Tropic Treasures by Ceramicraft.** Fish wall pocket. Brown & white, 9" long. With bubbles. $26-30.

Row 4

1. **Lefton.** Fish wall pockets & freestanding (pair) marked 218. Pink & blue. 7" long . With bubbles. $58-65 pair.
2. **No mark.** Fish (set of 2). White/green/black and white/yellow/black. 7-1/2" long. $24-30 set.

104

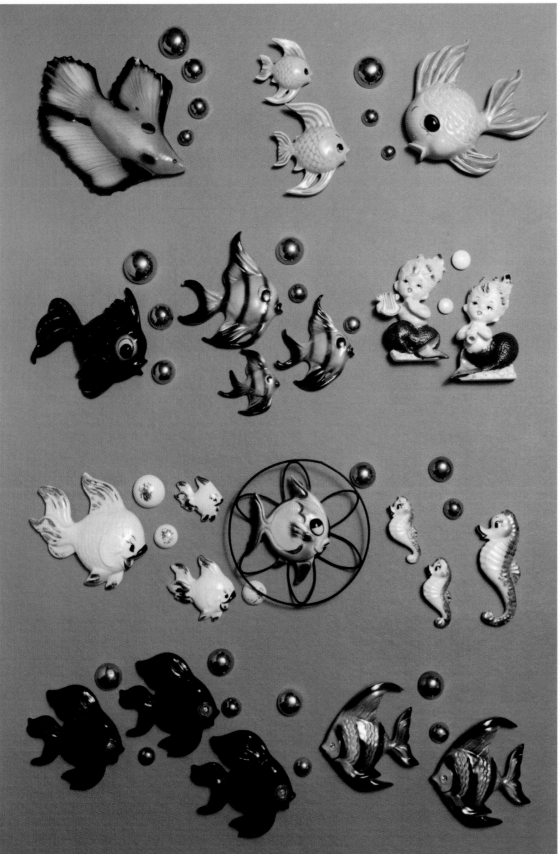

Row 1 (top, left to right)

1. **Erickson's Gy/wares, California.** Fish (Betta). Pink & black. 11-1/2" long. $40-45.
2. **No mark.** Fish (pair). Pink and blue. Small, 3-1/2" long, $4-8; medium, 5" long. $8-12.
3. **No mark, but believed to be Ceramicraft, San Clemente, California.** Fish. Pink and blue. 9" long. $18-24.

Row 2

1. **Ceramicraft, San Clemente, California.** Fish. Black & gold. 7-1/2" long. $24-28.
2. **Ceramicraft, San Clemente, California.** Fish (set of 3). Green & black, Large, 6-1/2" long; medium, 5" long; small, 3-3/4" long. With bubbles. $40-45 set.
3. **Bradley Exclusive, Japan.** Mermaids (pair). Green tails. 6-1/2" tall. $140-150 set.

Row 3

1. **DeForest.** Fish (set of 3). Yellow/white/gold. Large, 7-3/4" long; medium, 4-3/4"; small, 2" long. With bubbles. $50-55 set.
2. **No mark.** Fish in a frame. Blue/yellow/gold. 5" long plus frame. $18-22.
3. **DeForest.** Seahorses (set of 3). Bright pink/white/gold. Large, 7-3/4" tall; small 4" tall. $38-40 set

Row 4

1. **Ceramicraft, San Clemente, California.** Fish (three). Black & gold, jewel eyes, 6-1/4" long. $18-23 ea.
2. **Ceramicraft, San Clemente, California.** Fish, (two). Aqua and black, jewel eyes, 6" long. $18-25 ea.

Row 1 (top, left to right)

1. **No mark.** Seahorses & starfish (set of 3). Aqua & gold. Seahorse, 7-1/2" tall; starfish, 7" wide. $35-38 set.
2. **No mark.** Mermaid holding fish. Pink tail. 6-1/4" long. $45-50.
3. **No mark.** Fish (pair). Green mottled. 7-1/4" & 6-1/2" long. With bubbles. $20-26 pair.

Row 2

1. **Ceramicraft, San Clemente, California.** Fish (group of 3). Brown & pearl, jewel eye. 6-1/2" long. $18-23 ea.
2. **P1 mark.** Mermaid. Pearl & gold tail. 4-3/4" long. $35-40.
3. **CNC Los Angeles/Japan.** Fish (set of 3). Black/light blue/yellow. Large, 7"; medium, 6"; small, 3-1/4" long. With bubbles. $40-45 set.

Row 3

1. **Tropic Treasures by Ceramicraft.** Fish wall pocket. Pink & black. 9" long. $26-30.
2. **Gilner, California.** Fish wall pocket. Blue & white. 5-1/2" long. $22-24.
3. **No mark.** Mermaids (set of 4). Light green & gold tail, pink shells, and jewels. Large, 9" tall; with mirror, 5-1/2"; with harp, 5-1/2"; with arrow, 5-1/4". With bubbles. $180-190 set.

Row 4

1. **No mark.** Fish wall pocket. Black & pearl. 7-3/4" long. $15-18
2. **Kelvin Exclusives, Japan.** Seahorses (set of 3). Rose brown. Large, 7-1/2" tall; medium, 6-1/2" tall; small, 4-1/2" tall. With bubbles. $55-60 set.
3. **Duran's Royal, California.** Fish wall pocket. Yellow & gray. 8" long. With bubbles. $15-20.
4. **Lefton Exclusive, Japan.** Fish. Pink & yellow. 8-1/2" tall. $18-24.

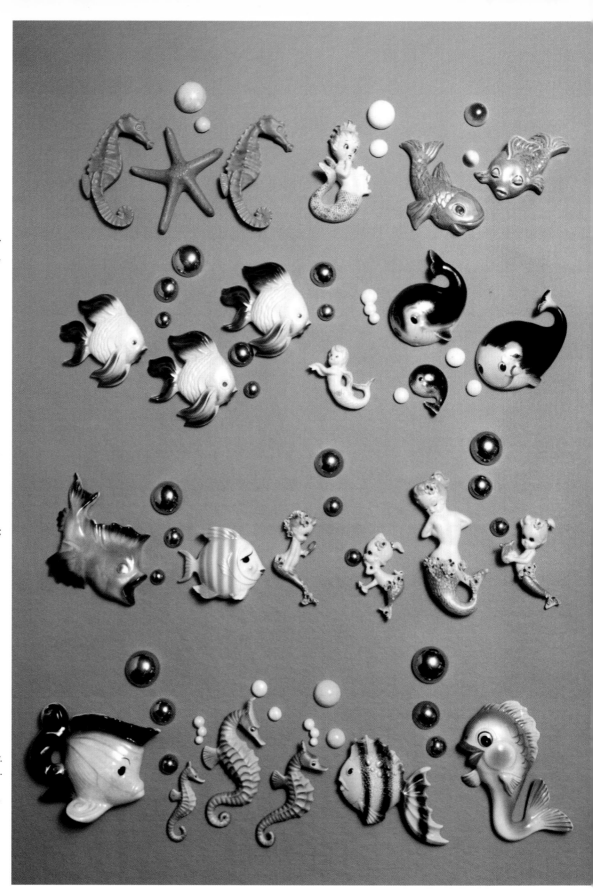

Row 1 (top, left to right)

1. **Josef Original, Japan.** Fish. Black & gold. 6-3/4" long. $40-45
2. **DeForest of California.** Fish (pair). Brown/gold/white. 5-3/4" long. With heart bubble. $38-45 pair.
3. **Freeman-McFarlin Original.** Fish wall pocket. Aqua & gold. 8-1/2" long. With bubbles. $26-30.

Row 2

1. **No mark, believed to be Japan.** Mermaids (set of 3). Light blue tails. Large, 5-3/4" tall; two small, 4-1/4" tall. $95-105 set.
2. **Japan.** Seahorses (set of 3), small red & silver sticker. Yellow/orange/green. Large, 7" tall; medium, 5-3/4"; small, 3-1/4". $35-40 set.

Row 3

1. **Ceramicraft, San Clemente, California.** Fish (four). Pink & black, jewel eyes. 6-1/4" long. $18-25 ea.
2. **Bradley Exclusive, Japan.** Mermaid. Pink tail. 6-1/2" tall. $70-75.

Row 4

1. **Duran's Royal, California.** Fish wall pockets (set of 3). Yellow/blue/black. Large, 7-1/2" long; medium, 6"; small, 3-3/4". $23-25 set.
2. **Bradley Exclusive, Japan.** Fish (pair). Black & white. 5" long. With bubbles. $24-28 pair.
3. **No mark.** Fish (1/2 of set). Pink/blue/silver/white. 6-1/4" long. With bubbles. $25-30

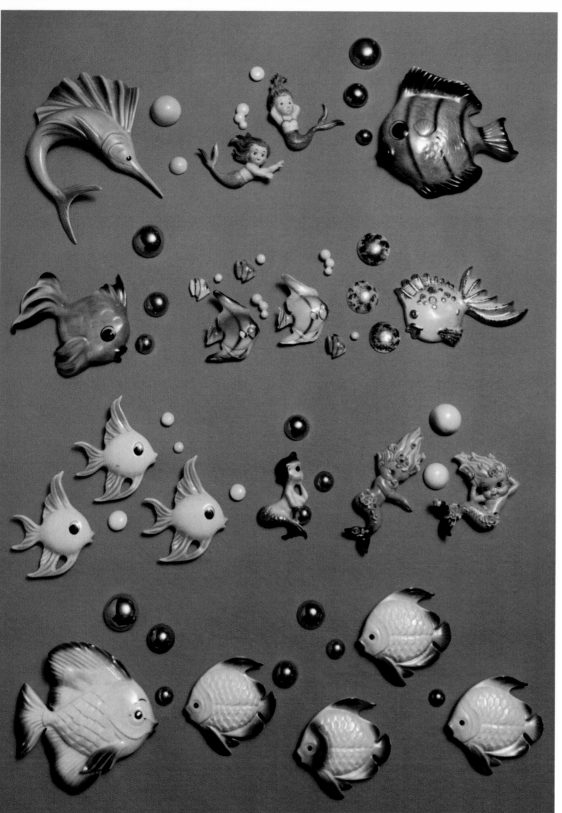

Row 1 (top, left to right)

1. **No mark.** Fish. Blue & light brown. 10-1/2" long. $24-28.
2. **Japan.** Mermaids, marked P-300 and P-360. Green tail. 5-3/4" long. $60-65 ea.
3. **Tropic Treasures by Ceramicraft.** Fish wall pocket. Aqua & black. 8-1/2" long. $36-40.

Row 2

1. **Tropic Treasures by Ceramicraft.** Fish. Pink & black, 7-1/2" long. $24-28.
2. **Norcrest Fine China.** Fish (set of 5). Blue/yellow/pink. Large, 4-1/4" tall; small, 1-3/4" tall. With bubbles. $25-28 set.
3. **No mark.** Fish. Blue & gold. 7-1/2" long. $18-22.

Row 3

1. **No mark.** Fish (set of 3). Aqua & white. 6-1/4" tall. $12-15 ea.
2. **Ceramicraft, San Clemente, California.** Mermaid, probably one of Ceramicraft's first mermaid designs. Green tail. 5" tall. $20-25.
3. **No mark.** Mermaids or water babies. Pink & black tail, shells, & jewels. 7-1/2" tall and 5-1/2" long. $30-35 ea.

Row 4

1. **Ceramicraft, San Clemente, California.** Fish. Brown & pearl. 8-1/2" long. $32-36.
2. **Ceramicraft, San Clemente, California.** Fish (set of 4). Brown & pearl, jewel eyes. 5-1/4" long. $22-26 ea.

Ceramicraft "Original Box"

Pictured below is a typical CERAMICRAFT gift box, containing a fish and three bubbles. Printed on the cover were the words, "Designed in CALIFORNIA by Ceramicraft - - to decorate the walls of your home." A description read, "#194-PEARL FISH W/3 GOLD BUBBLES PINK w/ BLACK TRIM. It had a price sticker indicating a regular price of $2.95 and a U.S.E. price of $2.24.

On the inside of the box is printed "HELPFUL SUG-GESTIONS" on the safe removal of the fish and bubbles. It reads, "Your genuine CERAMICRAFT creation is giftboxed for your convenience. The piece which you have chosen is glued to the cardboard tray for protection in transportation and for display purposes. The item is easily removed by soaking the tray in water for about ten minutes. Do not immerse the entire piece in water, just the cardboard tray. Do not try to pry the piece off with a sharp object, since it will damage the piece and might also crack or damage the glaze."

Also on the inside of the box, on the opposite side, the "Helpful Suggestions" continued as follows: "After the removal, dry the objects carefully. Select a suitable place on the wall where you intend to hang this wall decoration. Paste a small piece of adhesive tape on the wall, drive a small brad through the tape at an angle to ensure a proper flush hanging. The adhesive tape will prevent your plaster wall from cracking. If you desire our latest brochure showing other attractive and interesting gift items which we manufacture, write to CERAMICRAFT, P.O. Box 125, San Clemente, California. We will be only too happy to send you and your friends a copy.

Ceramicraft, San Clemente, California.
Fish: pink/black, 9" long. In original box. $50-75.

(Original Box)
DeForest of California, Duarte, California
Fish. Pink/white/gold. Large, 7-3/4" long; medium, 3-1/2" long; small, 2" long. In the Original Box, signed & decorated by DeForest of California. In many cases, the box was the only mark. $70-85.

DeForest of California, Duarte, California
Fish & fish soapdish. Pink/white/gold.
Fish, 9-1/2" long; soapdish, 8" long. In
Original Box: $120-130.

Japan
Seahorses. Yellow/green/orange. Large, 7" tall;
medium, 5-3/4"; small, 3-1/4". $55-65. Mermaids.
Green tail. 4-3/4" long & 6-1/4" tall. Small red & gold
sticker reads "Japan." Both are shown in original boxes
with undersea artwork. $175-185.

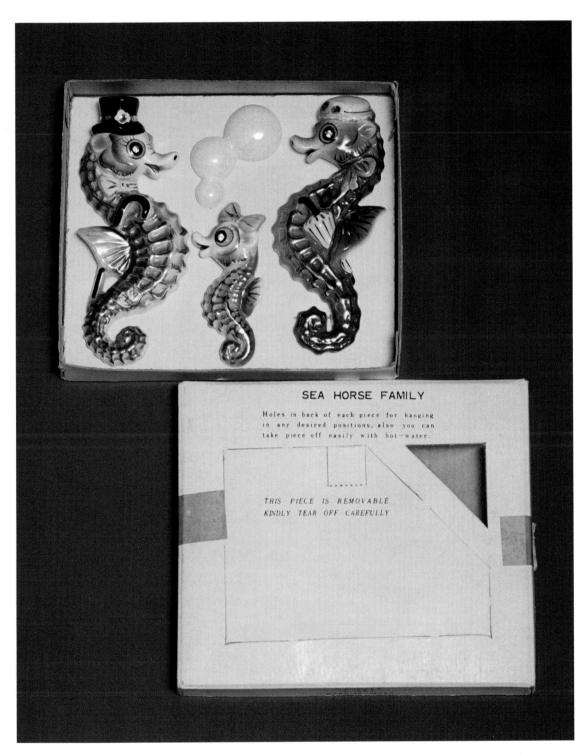

UCAGCO, Japan
Seahorses (set of 3) in original box. Large,
6"; small, 3-1/2". Jewel eyes. With bubbles.
$140-155 set.

**(Original Box)
Norcrest China Co., Japan**
Seahorses, marked P-999, in
original box. White & gold, jewel
eyes. Large, 6" tall; medium, 5-1/4";
small, 4". $45-48 set.

Japan
Mermaids (set of 3) in original box. White & gold
tails. With bubbles. $120-130 set.

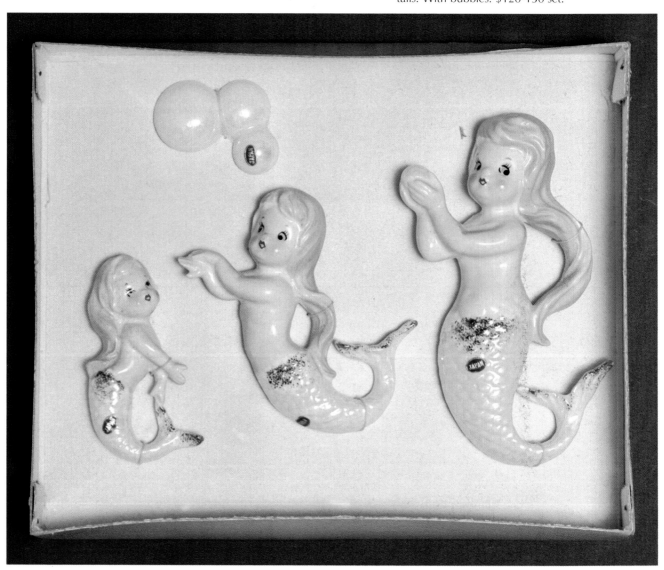

A Celebrity Fish ?

She had a special place in an Oscar-winning movie. That's right, I discovered a ceramic fish that made her debut alongside such luminaries and true "movie stars" as Tom Hanks, Kevin Bacon, and Ed Harris. The movie was Apollo 13. Did you see it? More importantly, did you see the cute little fish on the wall in the scene when a woman is coming out of the shower. I don't imagine many of the male readers of this book will have seen the wall decoration. You have to be a true "fish person" to spot such important things. If you missed it, I recommend that you either rent or purchase the videotape and enjoy this fine film again. And this time, check out the "fish moment." You can even do a stop frame when our little fish makes an appearance.

Section Two

Grouping Ideas

Other collectibles you may want to add to your collection of ceramic sea creatures, are *salt and pepper shakers, in* the shapes of fishes, mermaids, seashells, crabs and lobsters, etc. They are made in many colors and sizes and make a beautiful addition to your collection and arrangements. Look closely and you will see several pictured on the following pages.

Group Two
See Section One for individual pricing.

Group One
See Section One for individual pricing.

Group Three
See Section One for individual pricing.

Group Four
See Section One for individual pricing.

Group Five
Kay Finch, California. Seahorses & Sea Fan.
See Section One for prices. **Irene Smith, California**
Fish, 7-1/2" long $22-25 each

Group Six
Freeman-McFarlin Originals, El Monte, California. *See Section One for individual pricing.*

Group Seven
See Section One for individual pricing.

Group Eight
Freeman-McFarlin Originals. Fish above seahorse. $20-25. **No Mark.** Seahorses (set of 3). $55-60 set.
For all others see Section One for individual pricing.

Group Nine
See Section One for individual pricing.

Group Ten
See Section One for individual pricing.

Group Eleven
See Section One for individual pricing.

Group Twelve
See Section One for individual pricing.

Group Thirteen
See Section One for individual pricing.

Group Fourteen
Note: Large fish on right was made by ESP
Japan #4195. With 2 babies and bubbles $65-
70 set. *See Section One for individual pricing.*

Group Fifteen
See Section One for individual pricing.

Group Sixteen
See Section One for individual pricing.

Group Seventeen
See Section One for individual pricing.

Section Three

Decorating Ideas
With Your Collection
of Sea Creatures

Featuring World Famous Marine

Life Artist David Miller

About the Artist ...David Miller

Several years ago my husband and I acquired an exquisite print of a painting of ocean sea life flora and fauna. The painting was aptly named, "Vivid Splendor." It exuded the most vivid and vibrant colors I had ever seen, with a luminous, almost 3-D quality. We had to have it for our home. It was painted by a world famous environmental artist by the name of David Miller.

David Miller's signed and numbered limited edition underwater island seascapes and lush tropical landscapes are highly-prized by thousands of public and private collectors throughout the world. His exceptional work is available through MAUI ART, at 1-800-866-MAUI.

When I was writing this book I never dreamed that I would be able to include paintings by David Miller among my decoration ideas. In seeking to obtain permission to show you the print that I have in my home, and the way that I have decorated around it with a few of my sea creature collection, I discovered that David makes his home in Northern California, and that he had a studio not many miles from my home.

I was thrilled to meet with David and his lovely wife, Nancy. They were so gracious and they granted us permission to present a few of his wonderful paintings to you, along with our decorating ideas and suggestions. I hope you enjoy them.

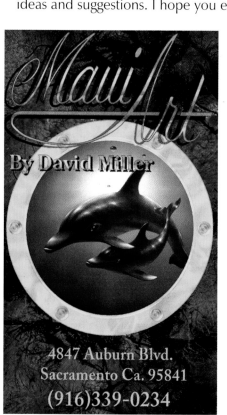

4847 Auburn Blvd.
Sacramento Ca. 95841
(916)339-0234

Wall Murals &

Other Decorating Ideas!!

There are many talented artists who have created wonderful underwater, tropical fish scenes, in oil, acrylic and watercolor paintings, lithographic prints, serigraphs and posters. You can add depth, dimension, brilliance and interest, by simply adding a few of your own ceramic fish.

For the artistic, creative and adventuresome, beautiful wall murals, or wall mural collages, utilizing multiple pictures, can be easily created by simply brousing through a few of the aquarist magazines, such as *Tropical Fish Hobbyist, Aquarium,* or *Aquarium Fish*, and select the pictures you like. Some wonderful fish are featured in these magazines. Simply cut them out and take them to a local copy center, that features color copying, and have the photo copied and enlarged to the size you want. Your pictures can be mounted, or framed, or simply hung with wallpaper glue. Add your favorite ceramic sea creatures, inside or outside of the picture, or both, and voilá, you will have created your own beautiful, decorative

To ARLEEN:
HAPPY FISHING!

David Miller

wall mural, or mural collage, for home or office.

Your local wallpaper store can be another excellent resource for new designs that may work well in decorating with your sea creature collection.

You may want to arrange and rearrange your collection into groupings, large and small. The decorating possibilities are endless. Let me show you a few ideas of what can be done with your sea creatures. They can be used to decorate:

.........a bathroom wall, or around the tub or shower
.........a kitchen wall, a bedroom wall, or in or around an aquarium
.........in or around an inside or outside swimming pool, spa, or hot tub
.........in the pool side dressing room
.........framed on an office wall
.........in your collectible displays

Just put your imagination to work and you'll find countless other ways to decorate while you are collecting - - and investing!

DAVID C. MILLER

ENCHANTED WATERS

123

125

Section Four

Just For Fun

The Infamous "Yellow Fish!"

Here's the one I promised to show you. This is the fish that didn't get away on my husband's "fishing trip." As homely and "plain vanilla" as it is, it still holds a treasured spot in my collection!

Closed
I've Gone Fishin'

Here's a sign for your door. **It's time for you to GO FISHING!!!**